Good Enough

Good Enough

40ish DEVOTIONALS FOR
A LIFE OF IMPERFECTION

KATE BOWLER
and JESSICA RICHIE

CONVERGENT

NEW YORK

Published in the United States by Convergent Books,
an imprint of Random House, a division of
Penguin Random House LLC, New York.

CONVERGENT BOOKS is a registered trademark
and its C colophon is a trademark of
Penguin Random House LLC.

All scripture quotations are taken from the Holy Bible, New
International Version®, NIV®. Copyright © 1973, 1978, 1984, 2011
by Biblica, Inc.™ Used by permission of Zondervan. All rights
reserved worldwide. (www.zondervan.com). The "NIV" and
"New International Version" are trademarks registered in the
United States Patent and Trademark Office by Biblica, Inc.™

LIBRARY OF CONGRESS CATALOGING-IN-PUBLICATION DATA
Names: Bowler, Kate, author. | Richie, Jessica, author.
Title: Good enough / Kate Bowler and Jessica Richie.
Description: New York : Convergent, [2022]
Identifiers: LCCN 2021044414 (print) | LCCN 2021044415 (ebook) |
ISBN 9780593193686 (hardcover) | ISBN 9780593193693 (ebook)
Subjects: LCSH: Perfectionism (Personality trait)—Religious
aspects—Christianity—Prayers and devotions.
Classification: LCC BV4597.58.P47 B69 2022 (print) |
LCC BV4597.58.P47 (ebook) | DDC 155.2/32—dc23
LC record available at https://lccn.loc.gov/2021044414
LC ebook record available at https://lccn.loc.gov/2021044415

Printed in the United States of America on acid-free paper

crownpublishing.com

2 4 6 8 9 7 5 3 1

First Edition

Book design by Jo Anne Metsch

*To those who loved me back to life when
I couldn't see the light.
Thank you will never be enough.*

—JESS

*This is for Jessica, who makes every dumb
dream come true. Let's open a zoo.*

—KATE

PREFACE

If you check your social media feed, the debate has been settled. Yes, you can be perfect. Other people are living beautiful, joyful, effortless lives. In fact, it's embarrassing that you haven't joined their ranks already.

Use this moisturizer. Lose those extra pounds. Smile at the cashier. Did you really give ten percent of your income to charity this year? Your grandma needs a card. I'm not sure you've forgiven your father. Your inbox is out of control. Did you finish that degree? There is a ninety-nine percent chance your children's photos have not been scrapbooked. Wait, what about that credit card debt? Your partner thinks you're selfish. Are you making the most of this?

And then what about the real stuff? You cheated. Or he did. You can't seem to find the person you wanted to be with or become that person yourself. You've been drinking again, and people are starting to notice. The program or job is a complete dead end. That teenager's addiction is eating you alive. Your mom is losing her memory and is miserable to care for. You wanted to be more: happier, healthier, wealthier, more grounded. But you're not.

We are living under the weight of the Perfectibility Paradigm.

Try harder. Do better. Other people are already at the finish line.

One of the most counterintuitive parts of the Christian tradition is its emphasis on progress when it doesn't believe in absolute perfection. Jesus alone is perfect. But we are asked to try and try and try again. We are required to walk toward God to the steady drumbeat of improvement.

We have entire faith traditions and denominations and institutions who come down on different sides of the debate surrounding how perfect we should expect to become. Some traditions, like Lutherans and Southern Baptists for example, double down on the language of justification, the account of how Jesus's death and resurrection saves us. And I mean, *saves us*. We were nothing. We were getting nowhere. Then *poof*. God rescued us from our innate brokenness. As the North African bishop Augustine said, *"Non possum non peccare."* I cannot not sin.

Other traditions (like, say, Catholics, Methodists, and Pentecostals) have a long practice of saying, "Yes, well, that's only the beginning." Being saved by God starts you on a path of sanctification—being changed by God—and you might even become close to perfect. Conveniently, this is called "Christian perfectionism." Progress is not simply expected but sometimes guaranteed.

Then there are all those who drink deeply from the wells of our modern self-help culture. They take a very precious truth about faith—that we can grow closer to God and become more fully human—and transform it into a capitalistic imperative. EVERYTHING is possible if you attend this seminar! Or buy this serum. Or commit to this new series of habits. This form of perfectionism argues that we are capable of anything at the right emotional, mental, and physical price, and admitting to anything else is just "low self-esteem." We are fine! No, not even that. We are perfect *just as we are.* Look within. We don't need to be saved at all. Everything you need is already inside of you.

Which one is it? Are we terrible? Perfectible? Already perfect?

We do not imagine that we will settle centuries of Christian debate about just *how* good we are, except that we believe it is somewhere between two poles: everything and nothing. Perfection is impossible, but transformation isn't. We can change a bit, if we really want to.

This is the choice embedded in every day from the moment we wake up. We will have to find enough momentum to reach for a faith that is never perfect, but good enough.

(Also, dear reader, please know that we have a sense of humor. So we are laughing every time we describe "good enough" as implying a gentle "meh." We love God. We simply know that we will not be joining a monastic order anytime soon and will have to figure out a reasonable spiritual plan given how much Netflix we are watching.)

WHAT KIND OF FAITH IS "GOOD ENOUGH"?

- A good enough faith will establish a sort of rhythm of life to sustain momentum. These are not an effort to ensure 7 Steps to Guaranteed Sainthood™, but rather to remind us that closeness with God is not just a question of belief. It is also in the small actions we can take.
- A good enough faith is not reaching for the impossible. We can't be everything to everyone, or even enough for ourselves. We're human.
- A good enough faith looks for beauty and truth in what's possible. No, not everything is possible. But we will hunt for the places where we can find an opportunity for a little more.

In taking this journey, you may realize that you were more committed to the Perfectibility Paradigm than you thought.

SIGNS YOU FELL INTO THE PERFECTIBILITY PARADIGM

- You look at others and fantasize about how your future self will also be amazing at [insert magical thing to be admired].
- You are deeply frustrated by yourself when you are not able to "stick with something."
- You stay too long in the self-help section at the bookstore, wondering if there is a secret to being better.
- You are confused about whether faith is a free solo experience. It is not. You are a group project.

TRUTHS TO START LOVING EVEN MORE

- We are made for interdependence.
- We are fragile . . . and so is everyone else. But we can learn to live beautifully inside of our limited bodies.
- Yes, our stupid, imperfect, ordinary lives can be holy.
- Life will break your heart, and there's nothing wrong with you if you know that.
- Sometimes joy and laughter and absurdity are the exact medicine we need, but also we need actual medicine. We love actual medicine too.

When life goes off the rails, we often believe we are the problem. But the reality is that so much is out of our control. You get sick. A friend dies. The baby's heart stops beating. The financial pressures are too much to bear. We have to learn to live inside of a life that may not be *perfectible*.

One way or another, we can't afford the lives we have—emotionally, spiritually, and financially. And guess what? There is no Best Life Now in sight.

So now what?

In this book, we hope to carve out the space between despair and hope, between believing everything is possible and nothing is possible.

We are on the lookout for beauty and meaning and truth in the midst of lives that didn't turn out like we thought they should. We can have lives where God breaks in and surprises us. We can learn to believe that we are blessed regardless of how our lives appear on social media or at high school reunions.

We can begin to feel less alone, more loved, and less judged when good is . . . enough.

HOW TO USE THIS BOOK

What follows are 40ish entries meant to be read as you sip your morning coffee or wait in the carpool line or while you're ignoring your partner at bedtime. You can read them in order or skip around or use them during

the forty days of Lent. *Trust us, no one is keeping score.*
Each includes a prayer or blessing because we believe in
blessing the crap out of people, and you look like you
could use it. Inside is also a simple prompt called a
Good Enough Step to nudge you toward action. No, not
every transformation is possible. But yes, there are some
things we can do to inch toward a deeper, richer, truer
kind of faith.

Let's begin. But before we do: A blessing for you, dear
one, as you embark on this joyfully mediocre journey[*]
toward, well, imperfection.

---

[*] We fundamentally hate the word *journey*. Journeys are for Frodo
Baggins and that 1980s band who took the midnight train going
an-yyyy-where.

A Blessing for a Joyfully Mediocre Journey

Blessed are you
who realize there is simply not enough
—time, money, resources.

Blessed are you
who are tired of pretending
that raw effort is the secret to perfection.
It's not. And you know that now.

Blessed are you
who need a gentle reminder that
even now, even today,
God is here,
and somehow,
that is good enough.

CONTENTS

CONTENTS

Good Enough

1

REGULA

(Pronounced "reg" like "regular." Not the way Jessica says it, like a rhyme for green-leafy "arugula.")

There's a feeling we get when we want to start something new. A little spark, a tiny flame has been kindled. There is some kind of desire or awareness rising. We start to hope for more, but we don't always know how to begin.

In our best moments, we notice that this feeling stirs up spiritual hopes. In a quiet moment. In a moment of awe. Sometimes in a moment of aching emptiness. We realize we want more.

Spiritual hunger, like other forms of desire, is fleeting. Hello! And goodbye! Now it's gone again. If we want our spiritual appetite to stick around, that will require a bit of attention. Our spiritual selves need encouragement. We need community. We need a hot minute alone. And we need a *regula*.

Regula means a "rule of life," but it is simply a *regular pattern of activities* that becomes more valuable over time because its structure creates a space for good things.

The most common understanding of the term *regula*

evokes images of a strict monastic life, where monks keep to a demanding daily schedule of grunt work and fervent prayer. Their days are divided into regular periods of communal worship, private prayer, spiritual reading, work, and sleep. Not everyone loves the rigors of a heavily scheduled life. Jessica Richie, co-author of this already beloved book, refuses to brush her teeth at the same time every day. Ever. She has to brush her teeth at completely different times each day or else, as an Enneagram Type Seven, she will surely die of predictability.

Sometimes we almost crave a tight regimen of rules only to suddenly lose momentum or decide that the cost is too high. If you have a history of dieting or joining exercise communities—CrossFit, SlimFast, Whole30, Peloton—you know how these moments feel. It is intoxicating until you can't keep up. Excitement quickly deteriorates into failure and shame. Perhaps you, like me, never last until the end of January with your New Year's resolutions. If so, I would strongly encourage you to be comforted by the earliest stories of rebellion against rules in the Christian tradition. In the sixth century, Saint Benedict had high hopes for the spiritual community he founded until his rules were deemed so unnecessarily strict that his followers tried to poison him.

Don't worry. He survived. And simmered down a bit. Benedict's main achievement became a set of rules that enshrined a spirit of moderation and balance, saying:

> "We hope to set down nothing harsh, nothing burdensome . . . As we progress in this way of life and in faith, we shall run on the path of God's commandments, our hearts overflowing with the inexpressible delight of love."

To be effective, a regula doesn't have to be hard; it only has to be regular. So don't worry so much today about whether you *want* to love God or whether you have all the spiritual feelings you think a better person would have. It's enough to say hello to the idea of trying.

A Blessing for Beginning a New Spiritual Practice

Blessed are we who are trying a new thing, though we can't quite see the whole of it. That's the beauty of the life of faith. We start in the middle, at the heart center of an unspoken desire to live into the glimpse we've had of You and of Your goodness.

Blessed are we who ask You to be the guide as we begin to build from here and create a stronger, more flexible rule of life. Trusting that you are trying to foster life in us.

Blessed are we who remember that we will fall short. We will fail, but that doesn't mean we are ruined. We simply pick up and begin again.

Blessed are we, willing to be beginners all over again.

A GOOD ENOUGH STEP

Regulas are not meant to be hard or heavy. We may have been given a story of what a faithful life is *supposed* to look like. We all know someone who seems to be effortlessly spiritual. I (Kate) had a friend whose morning ritual of thirty minutes of Bible study and silent prayer seemed so utterly natural to her that I always felt unmotivated by comparison. Don't I care about God? Don't I care about God *in the morning*? I got so stuck on the idea of this habit as the only true way to become spiritual that I needed to find an entirely different version.

What is something you can set down or let yourself off the hook for? Something that has made a life of faith seem impossible. Write it down on a piece of paper, then throw it away. Practice letting this expectation go so you can take up something gentler.

We thought it might be a nice reminder for you that not all habits are follow-through-able. Here are some of the things we have tried . . . and failed to do regularly. What would you contribute?

1. Not biting nails
2. Not throwing the alarm clock (or pressing snooze seven times)
3. Losing weight

4. Not talking about losing weight anymore (because, seriously, we can learn to love ourselves)
5. Flossing (apologies to our dentist friends)
6. Accepting email calendar invites
7. Drinking enough water
8. Canceling subscriptions (because, really, you haven't read that online magazine you subscribed to three years ago)
9. Reading for joy
10. Watching more edifying television (reality TV is just too entertaining)
11. Writing thank-you cards
12. Calling your mom, Jessica

2

BUOYED BY THE ABSURD

My grandmother was dying. It had been a long haul since her initial diagnosis and brutal treatments, and we were struggling under the weight of another painful truth: although she was not going to get better, she was also not going to face that fact. No late life lessons or awakenings in the face of her own demise for her, no sir. This was going to be hard until the end of the line.

My mom was always hovering nearby, waiting to see what she could do next. This went on for days and days and days.

One hospital day, my mom sat down to crack open her lunch and take a breather from keeping watch, only to discover that the meatballs she was looking forward to eating were frozen solid. She poked at them dolefully with a plastic fork, then nibbled around the edges. Rocks. Delicious frozen rocks. Suddenly the quiet hallways of the hospital were full of my mom's lightly hysterical giggling.

At that moment, one of my grandmother's friends popped her head in to see where the laughter was coming from. Her face tightened with disapproval.

"Is anyone with your mother?" she asked tersely, as if my mom had abandoned her post. Or insulted the sanctity of the space. Someone was *dying*. How *dare* anyone laugh about meatballs?

This is such a common feeling. I have a friend who lives in a poverty-stricken neighborhood, so she refuses to throw her children birthday parties. *How can we celebrate when others suffer?* Another friend lived in South Africa during apartheid and was ashamed to plan her wedding in the midst of such a painful national struggle for racial equality.

Is it okay to laugh when sadness surrounds us?

While all these people have good intentions, they are missing something important. Joy and sorrow simply coexist.

With all the misery at the hands of the Romans during first-century Palestine, Jesus attended a party. He didn't just attend . . . it was at this soirée where he performed his first miracle. The evening had been going so well until the couple committed the social blunder of running out of wine. Jesus could have simply given a rousing sermon: Enough revelry! Be grateful! Indulgence is the enemy! But instead, he took jars of water and transformed them into an even better wine than they had enjoyed to that point. The cheap house red became an expensive bottle of the finest Bordeaux. Even someone with a head cold would have been able to taste the difference. Another time, thousands of grumbling bellies surrounded Jesus. He didn't simply make enough for a small portion, but baskets of leftovers overflowed.

Later, when Jesus was resurrected from the dead, the first thing he did when he appeared to the disciples in the upper room was to ask if they had something to eat. This was a man who enjoyed a feast.

Under the weight of our grief, our shame, our pain or that of the world, we can convince ourselves that joy is the enemy. That to celebrate or feel happiness somehow mocks pain. But it is sometimes the opposite. Joy is the oxygen for doing hard things, as Gary Haugen says. He is the founder and CEO of International Justice Mission, an organization that frees people around the world from human slavery. The injustice he has witnessed firsthand would make even the sunniest heavy with despair. But Gary is the opposite. His levity is contagious—and exactly what sustains him to do the long, faithful work of justice.

When you are sinking under the weight of grief or falling prey to the fears that stalk your mind, try on joy for a change. Turn on the music and dance in your kitchen. Plan a road trip to the world's largest disco ball, prairie chicken, and chest of drawers for no reason at all. (Yes, I have seen them all and then some.) Bake a cake and have a party celebrating that it's Tuesday. Drop a surprise note and treat on a friend's doorstep. Try a cartwheel in the yard. Watch a show that makes you laugh. Ask friends to send you funny memes. Pull a lighthearted prank on your housemate. (Once Jessica taped the handheld faucet on the sink into the ON position so when her mom went to wash her hands, she got soaked. She laughed—the first time. She did not laugh the second or third time.)

Some people will try to tell you to just "choose joy," as if reframing your perspective will make things hurt less. I wish I could tell you joy was a magic formula. But, no matter how joyful you choose to act, joy does not erase the pain. Some things cannot be canceled out. But you are capable of a whole range of emotions that can coexist. Joy and sorrow. Grief and delight. Laughter and despair. Sometimes, the absurdity even keeps us afloat.

A Prayer for Finding Joy in Sorrow

God, I can't deny it, the way that sorrow catches up with me and forces me to pay attention. There is much to grieve, so much to lament in the world, in my life, in the lives of those I love. You have shown me again and again that I can look sorrow in the face, take its hand and talk things over, because it shows me what I love. It tells me what I don't want to lose.

God, I love that You lead me into that tender space where I can see the sadness for what it is, and I can see also what makes me want to fight hard for what I love. We are in this together, so dance me through it. Let's find some light in this day. Lead me to where I feel closer to You in my sadness and remind me that I never walk alone. Awaken me to the next step toward joy, so that what is a deliberate choice becomes a buoy, carrying me along a river of delight.

Dance with me, God. Show me the pleasures in the everyday loveliness of the world You created. Reveal what delights I can share, and the sadness I can ease. Do it again, Lord. Fill my heart with love for life and for others. That's where it starts, right where joy and sorrow meet. *Amen.*

A GOOD ENOUGH STEP

We are made for joy and delight and whimsy. But there is a discipline to this kind of joy, especially when we're not feeling especially cheery. Kate has been known to go to a thrift store, pick out an old painting, take it home, and paint a monster in the background. Or a dinosaur, if she's feeling extra spicy. Jessica once threw a Taylor Swift party where everyone had to dress up as their favorite Taylor Swift era (there are many to choose from) and lip-synch to her songs. Today, even if you aren't feeling very joyful, pick something absurd. Do it. *How do you feel?*

"I have been in Sorrow's kitchen and licked out all the pots. Then I have stood on the peaky mountain wrapped in rainbows, with a harp and sword in my hands."

—ZORA NEALE HURSTON, *Dust Tracks on a Road*

3

MOURNING A FUTURE SELF

Oh friend, if you were drawn to read this particular entry today, perhaps you are in that place where grief is what makes the most sense to you right now.

Because there is something that will now never be. There is an imagined future, something beautiful and dear to your heart, and it has dissolved before your eyes.

What is it that you grieve?

Perhaps your grief has a name. She is gone. He will never come back. The funeral is over, but the pain lingers. Perhaps you are grieving an event: an accident, an illness, a messy divorce. Maybe you are mourning a relationship that has come to an end with no possibility for forgiveness or reconciliation. Or perhaps you grieve for a marriage or relationship you still hope for, and work for, but one that has painted you into a corner.

Or is it someone close to you? Maybe you mourn for the relative with mental illness, a child who continues to struggle, or the loved one who will never be able to drive, work, or have the relationships that would make life feel full. Or maybe you lost an opportunity to do the right thing, say what mattered. Or perhaps you couldn't say goodbye.

I know that ache. It is a deep sadness that reverberates through our bones. We mourn not in general, but in particular. After all, love is in the details. It is, as Dr. Don Rosenstein says, "the loss of an imagined future." He is a clinical psychiatrist who works in a cancer center. An unexpected form of grief emerged for him when his son was diagnosed on the autism spectrum. He had to grieve the loss of who he'd imagined his son to be. He had to give up on the fantasy of a future where he and his son could hit tennis balls back and forth. Of course, his son is lovable and loved. But Don had to mourn his expectations and root around for a new dream of what it means to be the dad of his *actual* son, not just the son he thought he might have.

Loss requires us to reimagine hope. But before hope comes acknowledgment. Let us count not only our blessings, but our losses. That might sound "negative" to people accustomed to leaning on optimism, but there are good reasons for starting with a deep accounting of loss. Honesty allows us a moment to pause and take stock *before* we forge ahead.

Acknowledging "this will never be" is the precursor to imagining what might happen next. Without it, we may inadvertently find ourselves trapped in what psychologists call "identity foreclosure." As psychologist Adam Grant describes, we can get tunnel vision. We commit and recommit to a single vision of the future, shutting down any alternate plans and the ability to adjust. You wanted to be a parent, but infertility made it too difficult. You hoped for a long-term partner by this age, but they haven't come along. You were excited to help raise your grandkids, but then they moved away. We are forever being kept from an imagined future. And without honesty, we cannot first mourn that loss.

When you cannot have the future you imagined, let the tears flow. Let yourself mourn. Pour out your grief in all its truth, with all your power, in whatever form comes. With words or songs or talking with friends. Long walks or screaming into the void. Let it out.

Tell God the whole of it. Even though it hurts. And especially the honest, angry parts. Anger is our soul's sentry, put there to protect our boundaries and the vulnerabilities we carry.

"To everything there is a season, and a time for every purpose under heaven." (Ecclesiastes 3:1)

There is a time to mourn. Let it take up as much space as it needs. Your future self can wait.

A Blessing for When You Mourn
What Could Have Been

———

Blessed are you, friend, sitting among the shards of what could have been. It is broken now, that dream you loved, and it has spilled out all over the ground. Blessed are you, dear one, letting your eyes look around and remember all the hope your dream once contained. All the love. All the beauty. Blessed are you, telling your tears they can flow. Telling your anger it can speak. Blessed are you when mourning is the holy work of the moment, for it speaks of what is real. Blessed are you, letting this loss speak all its terrible truth to your soul.

Blessed are we who mourn, saying let us remain in grief's cold winter for as long as it takes, that mourning might be to our hearts the gentlest springtime. Let the thaw come slowly, so we can bear the pain of it and find comfort at each release. *Amen.*

A GOOD ENOUGH STEP

Ritual helps us mark important transitions. I have a friend who, after her divorce, held a funeral for her marriage. Another person held a memorial for who she was before a traumatic brain injury left her changed.

Plan a funeral for something you are grieving—an imagined future or the death of what could have been. Set aside a time and a place for your grief to be named and expressed. Write down its name on a small card, and set it out on a little table. Light a candle. Wear black, or a shirt that you can tear in half. Read a poem, play a song, or say a simple phrase like this one: "Oh light that once shone, you have departed. How I loved you. And how I miss you now that you are gone. I release you, and yet part of you will always be with me. Yet even as I hold the beauty of memory and the sadness of loss, I commit you now into the hands of God whose heart holds all that I don't understand. Amen."

"God pity them both! and pity us all,
Who vainly the dreams of youth recall;

For of all sad words of tongue or pen,
The saddest are these: 'It might have been!'

Ah, well! for us all some sweet hope lies
Deeply buried from human eyes;

And, in the hereafter, angels may
Roll the stone from its grave away!"

—JOHN GREENLEAF WHITTIER, "Maud Muller"

4

SHINY THINGS

teach in one of the great mainline seminaries in the world (if you don't mind me saying something so gauche), a bastion of American Methodism and a standard-bearer of the Protestant mainline in an era of declining vitality. And I got terribly sick when I was there, and I spent most of my time trying not to die, and they were pious and beautiful and soul-saving in every way.

I have always loved my job. It has always felt like the purest expression of who I am. I find much of my energy and my attention is devoted to a version of my career that, conveniently, suits me perfectly. So I have the kind of life that is perfectly suited to idolatry of the highest order.

Let me explain.

One of the defining features of cosmopolitan Protestantism is the sweet little promise—whispered even—that Christianity is not going to ruin your life. You can still love salty language (and I do) and feel justified by holding prevailing opinions (which I do) and have many mild to moderate faults that are not polite for me to mention. Its wonderful accommodation to modernity has liberated the church from a great many sins (Phariseeism, disembodied love, political acquiescence, etc.), but I'm afraid it has laid itself quite open to the glories of idolatry. And let me be clear, idolatry—which is to say, comforting false images of a true God—is the most fun in town.

There's a wonderful account in our tradition, in the book of Exodus, about our irresistible pull toward worship of the wrong thing. The Israelites have already been rescued from Egypt. They have been miraculously and ceremoniously yanked out of slavery and oppression. They are a people whom the Lord has saved and provided with all the food and water and sustenance they needed, despite much whining on their part.

They have been given a series of laws like "You shall have no other gods before me," and "You shall not make for yourself a graven image."

The people had been given two wonderful leaders: Moses, the intercessor, and Aaron, his brother and the high priest. He would tend to the religious needs of the people while Moses was up on the mountain, lingering with God.

Now, in the story, we are about to see Aaron do some spiritual improvisation. Moses is up the mountain receiving the rest of God's laws on Israel's behalf. Meanwhile, the people are getting impatient that Moses is "so long in coming down."

The Israelites say to Aaron, "Come make us gods who will go before us. As for this fellow Moses (who brought us up out of Egypt), we don't know what has happened to him."

Aaron told the Israelites to surrender their jewelry, then he whipped out an iron cast (I'd love to know where that miraculously came from) and smelted everything into a glorious idol. Later, when Aaron explains this to an irate Moses, he uses the most deliciously shoulder-shrugging explanation. He "threw it into the fire, and out came this calf!" (*How did that happen?!*)

It's not simply that the Israelites were wildly impatient and prone to epic forgetfulness. It's not only that they immediately fashioned a golden calf the minute that Moses was "too long in coming down." It was their defense. They argued that they were still, somehow, not violating the first commandment. After all, they did not create an image of a false God. They created a *false* image of the *true* God.

Welcome to your idols, people of Israel. *They aren't idols, I swear. It's still Yahweh. This is the festival of Yahweh, can't you tell?*

The golden calf brings home the fundamental issue for Christians who are not particularly worried about being apostates. At least not often. We are not unusually haunted by the specter of our salvation or in danger of being entirely unaware of our false pursuits. I work predominantly with pastors, and I have yet to hear any good sermons that come out strongly in favor of any of the exciting sins.

My sense is that we are more likely to be Judas than Peter. Peter denies God. Judas betrays him.

In other words, we are much more likely to do exactly what the Israelites have done: not to have a false image of a false God, but a false image of the true God. We take great comfort in our own version of God instead. Perhaps one that is composed of bits of things I already know are good and golden, things I melted into a god-like form. *Oh, is that an idol? It looked so familiar I hardly would have noticed.*

As Martin Luther famously wrote in his *Large Catechism,* "That to which your heart clings and entrusts itself is, I say, really your God."

An idol is like a flowering weed. It grows and spreads. Its blooms can fill a whole garden, even creeping over the edge and onto the lawn, without any cultivation. You don't even have to try, and it grows to take up every available nutrient in the soil, lightly choking out other, more tender, species. If it's lovely to look at, its sprawling tendrils often become too hard to yank out. And why bother? It looks like a garden. It looks JUST. LIKE. A GARDEN.

We are less likely to commit any of the very dramatic sins (murder! arson!). Instead, we are more likely to live comforting half-lives of faithfulness. The substitutions. Where we put in all the effort of declaring to be followers of Yahweh. Until we're not, as much.

There is a lovely book of advice for writers called *Turning Pro* by Steven Pressfield, which talks about how much easier it is to pursue a *version* of something than the real thing. Pressfield says that the biggest obstacle to great writing is the same for great living. It is to substitute a safer, lesser goal for the tough and exciting work you really ought to be doing. He calls this a "shadow career."

You are a teacher but it's less about the kids now and mostly about getting to the end of the day. Or you thought you wanted to be a parent and now you dream about being alone most of the time. Or you're humming other people's songs when you are too afraid to play your own.

The key, says Pressfield, is to ask yourself what your life is trying to point to. That's a wonderful and horrible thing to think about.

We are not apostates. We are idolaters. We fall in love with the things that are almost true. We start taking our gold and pouring it into a cast that we can shape with our own hands, one that inspires us and challenges us, but is not, necessarily, given to us by the one true God.

After all, what is idolatry except beautiful things that do not transform us?

A Blessing for Letting Go of the Things That Shine

Blessed are we, when the heart shudders to ask, is it me, Lord? Am I one who has chosen to follow a proxy? What does my life point to? When I look at the decisions I make and the ways I spend my time and my money, what is it that I love? What does the evidence tell me about the cause that I care for the most?

Blessed are we who cringe at the thought of betraying You, the lover of our souls.

Blessed are we who have caught ourselves walking the road toward self-justification, who pause to ask, is it really You, God, I worship? The Immortal, the Ancient of Days, yet no stranger because You make yourself known.

Oh, how blessed are we who lay it all out before You, oh God, asking to be awakened to our lives as You see them. Asking for the inward renovation that will tear down anything false we worship, and for the outward turning that will make every aspect of our life point to You.

Blessed are we, looking for the transformation that has begun, one delight at a time.

A GOOD ENOUGH STEP

What do your major life choices point toward? Your relationships . . . your kids . . . your career . . . your hobbies . . . the places
you want to travel?

What is the most beautiful thing you can say about your life
when you look at the evidence?

You want to love people.

You want to challenge deeply held ideas.

You want to take risks.

Write it down. Be clear. Be specific.

What is a core truth of your life, the straightest arrow you
can imagine finding there? Now ask yourself: *Is it aimed too
low?*

"Sometimes, when we're terrified of embracing our true
calling, we'll pursue a shadow calling instead. That shadow
career is a metaphor for our real career. Its shape is similar, its
contours feel tantalizingly the same."

—STEVEN PRESSFIELD, *Turning Pro*

5

BUILDING A GOOD DAY

I love to openly begrudge a good sermon analogy. If someone begins to describe God's love as a lesson she learned by pushing her daughter on a swing, I vow never to visit a playground again. Did you learn freedom from sin during a skydiving lesson? But no lessons learned about the odds of falling precipitously to your death? Good luck leaving the sanctuary without me bringing that up.

But this one stuck.

An old Mennonite pastor was at the pulpit explaining the importance of time spent with God, and he took out a wide-mouthed mason jar. He began to drop stones of various sizes to the bottom. Big. Small. Smooth and jagged. *Plonk. Plonk. Plonk.*

"Notice what happens when you put them in randomly," he said dramatically, and the jar quickly filled up to the top with dozens of stones left over. We shrugged.

"Now notice what happens when you put in the large stones first," he observed sagely, and I started to pay attention.

The largest stones anchored the bottom, then the medium stones, then the smallest stones filled in all the cracks. Presto! All the stones fit snugly in the jar as each settled. And, with the Mennonites around me—which is to say, people deeply impressed by good, common sense—I rolled my eyes and agreed it was the best thing I'd seen in months.

For some people, the idea of prioritizing how to spend their day is very intimidating. I vividly remember my lonely grandfather, whom I loved more than butterscotch, explaining how the day felt absolutely interminable. In my recent conversation with author Mary Pipher, she wholeheartedly agreed: a single day can feel impossible to wrangle into shape. As she got older, her friends were dying and her role was changing rapidly, and all the familiar work of parenting and caregiving and working had given way to an entirely amorphous existence. She, like the Mennonite pastor, decided that the trick was to treat the day as something to prioritize.

First, she decided, there would have to be a walk. She would listen to the birds, *no matter what*. "We need to learn how to structure a day that is rich in meaning and joy-producing activities," she writes. "How we spend our time defines who we are. There is no magical future. Today is our future."

A day is a limited thing. It is a mason jar with only so much room to spare. So, as the adage goes, first things first.

It will take some time for you to decide what the Big Stones and the Small Stones should be. Some seasons of our lives are overwhelmingly crowded, and if that's the case for you just now, I completely understand. Maybe you can take a single moment, just breathe and ground yourself in the remembrance that you are a complete delight. Just this could be your touchstone.

The best days will have room for the Big Stones. That doesn't mean that everything has to happen in the morning. There are two dozen self-help bestsellers at any moment ready to explain to you that you can solve the problem of bad days by conquering your mornings. Sorry. Some people like to sleep in and, again, good luck trying to get Jessica to do anything on a fixed schedule.

The structure of a good day is simply this: your biggest loves find their way in. God. Friends. Meaning. Family. Take some real unhurried time to reflect on how a spiritual practice might pop into your day. When is it practical for you? What is your preference? A night owl might choose to set aside a bedtime moment for her spiritual practice. Another might find that lunch is best. Either way, you will need a regular reminder to look for God.

And when your day is getting too stuffed, stop. Notice what is happening. Ask God for help, and look for the coming of Love that renews and restores the goodness.

Perhaps you have serious limitations—a health condition or too much work or caregiving to do. My friend with leukemia recently told me that she began to see each day as capable of only three things. Take a shower. Call a friend. Make lunch. Others have forty thousand things that must be done. To be human is to accept that we are limited and the more honesty we have about that, the better.

If we want to build a good day, we can start with just that. One day. One jarful at a time.

A Prayer at the Start of the Day

Dear God,

Help me stop, for I am likely to keep doing all the things I usually do. And in that stopping, meet me here, in the beauty of all Your incredible mercy and goodness. And in doing so, remind me again that of course You're here, You're listening, because that is who You are.

You are the kindness that runs to find me wherever I have wandered off to. You are the faithfulness I don't have enough of. You are my safe harbor in the midst of the storm. And in that quiet place, speak gently to me of what needs to change in order for Your freedom to free me, Your love to care through me, and Your faithfulness to strengthen me.

Through our Lord Jesus Christ, Your Son who lives and reigns with You in the unity of the Holy Spirit, one God, for ever and ever.

Amen.

A GOOD ENOUGH STEP

Think about the day you'll have tomorrow. Is there anything you can cross off or kick down the road? Don't crowd your day.

Find a prompt to remind you to let God in, e.g., a pebble in your pocket, a sticky note on your bathroom mirror, a rubber band bracelet.

What are your big loves? Allow them to take up space.

Then, do it again tomorrow. One good day at a time.

"Like sands through the hourglass, so are the days of our lives." —Kate's favorite soap opera

6

SMALL THINGS, GREAT LOVE

I was a good musician, but a terrible music student. I was deeply invested in wanting to learn the cello, but not terribly invested in practicing. I would show up at my lessons with my teacher, Adeline Muller, and do a lot of talking and impressive gesturing at the music. And Adeline, for her part, continued to act like I was on the cusp of getting better, despite all evidence to the contrary. She showed up, so I showed up. That was Adeline's way.

Adeline always showed up. Every Sunday morning, she would play the piano and our small Mennonite church would sing along. If you've ever heard a small congregation singing, it is . . . underwhelming. Someone is always working too hard on the high notes, the rest are struggling to keep time, and the pianist acts like the conductor and the orchestra. It's wonderful and exhausting and important because it makes everyone show up, especially God.

One day, Adeline's husband of fifty-six years passed away. He was a wonderful man with a fabulous mustache and a huge smile, and we were all heartbroken.

The next Sunday, we expected to forge ahead in the service as best we could without our faithful accompanist. But there was Adeline. At the piano.

"What are you doing here?" someone exclaimed.

She paused, as if confused by the question.

"I was on the calendar."

There are many acts of great love that are great because they are massive, monumental, and earth-shattering. And some are great because they are incremental. Each small act adds up to something really spectacular.

Small acts, great love.

There's actually a saint of small things. Her name is Thérèse, born in 1873 to a middle-class family in France. She lost her mom to breast cancer when she was four years old and grew up as an emotionally sensitive and spiritually interested child. As a teenager, she decided she wanted to become a nun and joined a group of contemplative nuns living sheltered from the world. She spent her years praying, serving, and writing inside those walls.

Her life, however, was short. Like many women of her generation, Thérèse died young, passing at age twenty-four of tuberculosis. There is nothing particularly extraordinary about her life, except the remarkable way that she decided to respond. When she learned that she would die, she decided that her ordinary life (with its limited scope and span) would be lived with limitless love. She called it "the little way."

"Love proves itself by deeds, so how am I to show my love? Great deeds are forbidden me. The only way I can prove my love is by scattering flowers, and these flowers are every little sacrifice, every glance and word, and the doing of the least actions for love."

When someone in her community would behave in a way that was ungracious or even petty and mean, Thérèse would double down and respond with even greater love and graciousness. She felt that it freed her.

We are often taught that our lives must be big to be remembered. But what if it was enough to scatter flowers? To make small sacrifices? Instead of mythologizing the rich and famous, let's pause to celebrate all those of us who walk the little way. Blessed are you who show up because you're on the schedule.

A Prayer for the Courage to Love Small

Dear God,

Bless me with a radical love, inventor of love. And may that love overflow onto, into, and through me. Flood me with Your kindness, generosity, and compassion, so that I may be Your hands and feet in the world.

Help me to remember that love isn't always in grand gestures or extravagant gifts, but in the small, faithful acts. Help me to remember it is in the showing up, in the work behind the scenes, in doing that which won't get us recognition. The one who is the first in and last out. The generosity of time, resources, spirit. The one who leaves flowers in her wake. This is the long faithfulness that can change the world.

God, bless me in this Little Way, to be able to do small things with great love. One small action at a time, until it's a bridge—with a span that reaches from my little life to Yours with each act of love. And when I screw up or forget or grow weary, bless me with the courage to begin again. Loving and loving again. Being changed by Your love and transforming the world one little act of love at a time. *May it be so.*

A GOOD ENOUGH STEP

The early church in Galatia debated about what makes someone *Christian* enough. Is it eating the right food? Wearing the right clothes? Hanging out with the right people? Obeying the rules enough? Paul quashes the argument by telling them: "What matters is something far more interior: faith expressed in love" (Galatians 5:6). Let this verse be yours for the day, or the week, or the month. Write it on a sticky note and put it on your mirror or desk or on your front door. Let the words wash over you. Meditate on how your small acts of love embody a greater faith.

"Life is mostly froth and bubble,
Two things stand like stone,
KINDNESS in another's trouble,
COURAGE in your own."

—ADAM LINDSAY GORDON, "Ye Wearie Wayfarer"

7

ASLEEP ON THE JOB

W hy are you so afraid?

An innocuous question if you have an irrational fear of, say, bunnies.

But for the disciples, there really was something to fear. They climbed into a boat with Jesus, something they had done hundreds of times before. At least four of them were seasoned fishermen, as were probably their fathers and their father's fathers before them. They had favorite fishing spots, knew the coastline like the backs of their hands, and could handle the boat in even the worst of weather. Or so they thought.

Jesus soon fell asleep on a little pillow. (I find this detail so delightful. *Does he drool? Does he snore? What does Jesus dream about?*) Then a storm came out of nowhere. Waves crashed into the boat; water spilled into the bow. The wind grew so strong they might have had splinters from white-knuckling the edge. All the while, Jesus napped.

The disciples seemed to admonish Jesus when he woke, "Don't you care if we drown?"

I wonder how often we have the same thought. *Do You not care? Where are You? Why have You allowed this? Have You hidden Your face from me? Are You punishing me?* Where is God when marriages fail and families crumble, when miscarriages and diagnoses, loneliness and depression take everything? We are God's children! Shouldn't we get something better when Jesus is *right there*?

God seems asleep on the job.

Then, with mere syllables, Jesus makes the water as still as a bathtub.

The disciples can't believe their eyes. Their jaws drop with wonder. They whisper to one another, "Who is this? The winds and the water listen to him."

"Why are you so afraid?" Jesus asks, getting right to the point.

To understand Jesus's question, we have to remember what the disciples knew about him thus far. At this point, Jesus has multiplied the disciples' fish, cured a man of leprosy, healed a paralyzed man, grown a man's arm back, healed the centurion's servant, raised a man from the dead, expelled demons, and restored sight to the blind. All before the disciples' very own eyeballs.

Jesus might have said, instead: "I thought you knew me."

Fast-forward to after Jesus's death and resurrection. The disciples are still . . . incredulous.

The man they had followed and loved, sat beside and eaten with, had been murdered in front of them and was now missing from his tomb. But there they were, headed out of town toward Emmaus, getting out of Dodge. A stranger began to walk with them, asking what they were discussing. A little confused that the stranger didn't know what had happened, they told him, "We had hoped he was the one . . ."

After all the miracles they had witnessed, the teaching they had heard, the whispers of his identity they had believed, they still believed that Jesus had let them down.

They didn't get it on the boat that day as Jesus silenced the wind and shut up the waves. They didn't get it when the news spread of Jesus resurrected from the dead. And they don't get it as Jesus walks beside them.

Who is this? they wonder. *We had hoped he was the one . . .*

How often in our own lives do we have a picture of who we want God to be? The ways we expect God to act. The miracles we want God to perform. The storms we've asked God to calm.

We had hoped he was the one who would eradicate the pandemic.

We had hoped he was the one who would reverse dementia. Shrink the tumor. Save the marriage. Erase the mental illness. Give us a baby.

We had hoped he was the one who wouldn't lead us *into* storms.

But instead, this is our God. The one who calls us to love the stranger and foreigner and enemy. The one who leads us into chaos. The one who heals some but not all.

Jesus is the one who dies and who is resurrected. And

the one whose presence remains but whose absence is always before us in this broken world. We marvel at the God who loves us and stays by our side, regardless of how little we understand or how often we wonder if our savior is asleep.

A Prayer for When God Seems Absent

Oh God, comfortable would we be if You gave us formulas and answered prayers and realized hope. But You call us beyond comfort.

But God, life upends us. We face divorce or miscarriages, financial struggles or job insecurity, and the people we love are tossed about by disease or loneliness or homelessness or addiction.

We are afraid. We don't have adequate answers. And sometimes we can't find You.

Or, we can't find the person we hoped You would be.

May we learn to trust that You aren't asleep on the job. That You haven't forgotten us. That You are as near to us as our very breath. Give us the courage to press on. To suffer with hope that You have overcome the world.

May again and again we be awed by Your presence. That even when we feel like we've hit rock bottom, may we recognize we have fallen into Your arms because there is no place so deep or so dark or so scary that Your presence cannot reach.

In the name of the One who can still the seas with mere words, *amen.*

A GOOD ENOUGH STEP

Let it surface—that fear that is just below the surface, masquerading as frustration or irritability or tension. Let it come forward to your mind and sit with it awhile. Then put it into a prayer—something very specific and simple that says, "God, please take over all of this, just for today." Rest.

Amazement, or *thau-ma-zo,* is a word Luke uses thirteen times in his Gospel. It describes crowds' incredulousness and wordlessness at Jesus's miracles or teachings.

But the most notable instance is when Jesus himself is awestruck by someone's faith. A Roman soldier requests healing for his servant and tells Jesus to not bother heading all the way to his home—he is not worthy of his presence—"But say the word, and my servant will be healed." The soldier trusts that with mere words, Jesus can perform the miraculous. Jesus responds with wonder: "I have not found such great faith even in Israel."

The centurion—a Roman!—has faith in Jesus's power and person and words. Faith that leaves Jesus wonderstruck. Faith that evades even Jesus's closest friends. We all have moments of deep belief and deep mistrust. Think back to a moment when your faith would have wowed Jesus. Something small or big. You believed.

8

WHEN GOOD THINGS
BECOME BURDENS

Let's say you've started a new spiritual practice. You're praying a bit more. You've even read *multiple entries of this book*. Wonderful! Or if you haven't, thank you for humoring me. I'll proceed regardless . . .

Let's assume that we are aiming to partake in some kind of spiritual act to guide us, sustain us, and help us live the life to which we have been called. Super. What could possibly go wrong? Well, two things. The first, perhaps most common, is that we are too lax. We forget or don't take it too seriously, and we never see the benefit of sticking with it. But, for some of us, we take rules too seriously—a rule becomes a law.

Let me give you an example. My friend Rachel grew up as a Hutterite, in that lesser-known Christian tradition (a spiritual cousin to the Amish and Mennonites) dedicated to communal living and devoted to simplicity. She grew up with the expectation that all prayer had to be done kneeling. At church and at home, she got on her knees to talk to God. But one night she suffered a burst appendix and was rushed to the hospital. She lay awake that night convinced she was going to die, and, terrified, tried to climb down off the gurney to pray. But she couldn't. She was tied in to IV fluids, and suddenly the thought occurred to her: *I'm going to die here, and I won't be ready. I can't ask for forgiveness and clear my conscience. I'm lying here, and God can't hear me.*

Now, regardless of whether you're the kind of person who has a lot of spiritual rules or none at all, we can see what happened to Rachel's thinking: the rule was originally designed to inspire humility. But the rule applied absolutely had become oppressive. Of course, God could hear her. But Rachel couldn't believe that unless she was on her knees.

There are plenty of ways in which we vest rules with too much power. Our ideas become so rigid that they are held up over all other considerations. We adopted them thinking that they could help us live, but our rules can't anticipate every circumstance, or meet every rising need. They just aren't flexible enough, smart enough, or compassionate enough. After all, a rule can't see you, or know you, or respond to you.

We might not think we are the kind of people who have a lot of rules, but I bet there are some lurking around. The billions of dollars poured into the health and wellness industry are designed to create a sense of urgency around new rules that "guarantee" your well-being. Maybe you were told that you are not "allowed" to eat after 8:00 P.M. Or that emptying your inbox was the only way to achieve organizational efficiency. (And if you are old enough, you can remember there was a time when you didn't *have an inbox*. And now it may rule the universe.) You can see the devolution from "Hey, that's a neat idea!" into an oppressive regime. You have been boxed out of your humanity by all these suggestions that seemed good at first glance.

A rule that takes on absolute power becomes a blunt instrument—something that loses the purpose for which it was created. Any rule or ideology is only useful, helpful, and salutary if it is under the authority of a higher law, the law of Love. And that law has in fact been established from the foundation of the world. God is Love.

This is the beautiful and central truth that grounds us when we seek to create practices that sustain life: God is alive. We seek a person, not a principle. The spiritual life you create is the space where God appears to you with the blessing that is for you.

And here's the amazing thing. The little habits we create with God's guidance will actually be made to fit us. Fit me. Fit you. The particular you, in this particular moment.

Jesus said: "Take my yoke upon you and learn of me . . . my yoke is easy and my burden is light" (Matthew 11:29–30).

A *yoke* is a carved piece of wood that is made to fit over the neck of a farm animal so it can pull a cart or wagon. If the yoke doesn't fit properly, it will chafe and the animal won't be able to do its job. A good yoke wouldn't be labeled GENERIC OX. It would be made for that body, the slope of his shoulders, the breadth of her back.

I know it's not very comforting to imagine ourselves as farm animals, but we know that we all carry burdens. We carry our lives on our backs. We need practices that fit us, that settle against the shape of our lives with ease.

Then the point of spiritual practice is not simply carry more, try harder, do better. It fits. It's easy. As Jesus says, "It's light, I swear."*

* All starred translations courtesy of Kate Bowler, who joyfully forgot all her Koine Greek in college. *Sorry, Dr. Overman. You tried. I know you tried.*

A Blessing for When You Want to Be Faithful but Don't Know Where to Start

---

God, sometimes following You feels strict, confining, like You're trying to steal joy from my hands. I long for the sweetness of Your presence and to live like You ask. But it feels too hard. Like I'm being held back. Like You want me to change beyond what I'm capable of. Faith has been wielded as a weapon against me and people I love. And I don't measure up to those exacting standards.

But You say that Your yoke is gentle and easy. And if that is true, may I see these small habits as opening a space for transformation. That instead of building walls around me, You erase the barriers I've built around who You are and how I should respond. You are not the judge on the sidelines, but You take me by the hand and guide me gently. And it is here that You promise rest.

Help me to see the gentleness with which You guide. Lead. Teach. God, make it sweet and doable. *Amen.*

A GOOD ENOUGH STEP

Prayer doesn't always come easily. Especially if you wonder, *Am I doing this right? What exactly is this for?* Start small by praying a psalm—a collection of prayers of lament, joy, celebration, collective grief. Pray the words of Psalm 13 if you're feeling forgotten by God. Pray Psalm 55 if you are feeling anxious. Pray Psalm 91 if you need encouragement. Borrow the words of the psalmists, remembering that God can handle a whole range of our emotions.

EXCITINGLY ABSURD RULES

In Arkansas, it is illegal to pronounce *Arkansas* incorrectly.

It is illegal to build, maintain, or use a nuclear weapon within Chico, California, city limits.

In Connecticut, a pickle fit for human consumption should bounce if dropped from a height of one foot.

In Gainesville, Georgia, it is against the law to eat fried chicken with a knife and fork.

In Marion, Oregon, ministers can't eat garlic or onions before delivering a sermon. (They might be onto something.)

You may not own more than 110 pounds of potatoes at one time, if you live in Western Australia.

9

THE FOUNDATION

I am self-made. Didn't anyone tell you? I brought myself into the world when I decided to be born on a bright Monday morning. Then I figured out how cells replicate to grow my own arms and legs and head to a reasonable height and size. Then I filled my own mind from kindergarten to graduation with information I gleaned from the great works of literature. I am basically Matt Damon from the movie *Good Will Hunting*. I'm a stand-alone genius of self-creation. It's incredible.

I'm joking, but sometimes it feels like the pressure we are under. An entire self-help and wellness industry made sure that we got the memo: we are supposed to articulate our lives as a solitary story of realization and progress. Work. Learn. Fix. Change. Every exciting action sounds like it is designed for an individual who needs to learn how to conquer a world of their own making.

It's hard to remember a deeper, comforting truth: we are built on a foundation not our own. We were born because two other people created a combination of biological matter. We went to schools where dozens and dozens of people crafted ideas and activities to construct categories in our minds. We learned skills honed by generations of craftspeople. We pray and worship with spiritual ideas refined by centuries of tradition. Almost nothing about us is original. *Thank God.*

It reminds me of the account of creation in Genesis. With mere syllables, waters split, life sprouts from the dirt, fish leap from the sea, peacocks get their feathers and zebras, their stripes. With a divine mud pie, God shapes and molds us in God's likeness. Skin stretches around bones as they crackle into place. Veins and arteries and nerves create complicated, invisible roads just below the skin's surface. God breathes oxygen into lungs in an instance of divine CPR. I love picturing that God, the only One who can create out of nothing—ex nihilo. God, who set the cornerstone of our lives and our faith, laid the first brick. The Master Builder whose carefully poured foundation is what we build on top of now. It certainly feels like a template for the rest of our experience.

When I was really sick and worried about dying too young, I kept trying to picture how much my son would remember. Would he remember my laugh? Would he know how it felt every morning when I pulled him under the covers and we talked about our hilarious dreams from the night before?

I thought about him all the time. When do children develop long-term memory? How much am I in *there* . . . his mischievous mind, his evil laugh. Then one day, my psychologist said something wonderful. He said: "Kate, you're in there. The foundation is the part that doesn't show."

Whether it is our parents, our teachers, mentors, friends, churches, or neighbors, people have been pouring into us. We are standing on a foundation. It should come as an incredible relief. Our only job is to build on what we've been given, and, even then, even our gifts we can trace back to the creativity, generosity, and foresight of others. *Thank God we are a group project.*

A Blessing for the Caregivers

Blessed are you, the care-ers, bone-tired from doing for others what you would love someone to do for you. Blessed are you, pouring yourself out day after day.

You are seen—in your struggles and kindnesses and missteps. In your faithfulness and love. What you have poured out has gone deep to the foundation that will last forever. You've created a bedrock of love.

Yet, dear one, blessed are you when you see that it is time now to take some rest. Time to be renewed and strengthened. Awakened to see and welcome with anticipation what's next. Blessed are you who recognize that not everything has to be done right now, and not everything has to be done by you. Close your eyes and see them all, the army of those who have cared for you in the past, who have fought for you, who have loved you well. And drink it in, creating a pool of gratitude that swells inside. For blessed are you, having received, and having loved, who can walk around with a thankful heart. *Amen.*

A GOOD ENOUGH STEP

Whose foundation are you standing on? Here is a list that may spark some names.

Doctors and nurses
Lab workers and paramedics
Family and friends
Teachers and mentors
Pastors and chaplains
Neighbors and community organizers
Grocery clerks and truckers
Police and firefighters
Cleaners, landscapers, and builders
Poets and writers
Inventors, scientists, and researchers
Musicians and composers
Teammates and co-workers
Charitable donors
Anybody doing their job competently (hooray!)
People with power who stayed kind somehow

Take a minute to whisper a word of thanks (or, if you are able, send them a note of gratitude).

"If I have seen further it is by standing on the shoulders of giants." —ISAAC NEWTON, letter to Robert Hooke

10

WHEN YOU ARE EXHAUSTED

Back in Manitoba, Canada (where Kate is from), winters are cold and dark and seem to last from October to May. There is lots of hockey and ice fishing on lakes on which you are certain large vehicles should not be driving. The snow sticks to your eyelashes, and 20 degrees below freezing is relatively balmy. To cope, I turn to candles, fireplaces, friends, and industrial-strength, goose-feather-filled parkas, and long walks at night to look at the stars. As I lean back and look up at that inky expanse, edged by the silver of the birch trees, the sky becomes a benign space where ideas effortlessly come and go. And, eventually, something stirs and busies itself within me, doing some kind of mysterious interior repair. I become a little more myself.

In our everything-must-be-done-fifteen-minutes-ago culture, every last ounce of effort has been expended, breathed out, spent. This exhaustion is not so much a place, but a signpost. It gives us useful information and tells us what to do next, but first we have to inventory. It's usually only in retrospect that I see how depleted I have actually become. How much I need a break.

The self-help industry would have you believe that whatever your problem, it can be fixed with a little more effort. *Maximize your workday! Have a miracle morning! Exercise for thirty minutes every day! Have you taken your daily apple cider vinegar shot?* (Pro tip: apple cider vinegar is better ingested in the form of a salad dressing. Not a shot glass.)

I recently read an article meant to inspire busy mothers by lifting up an eighteenth-century paragon of female virtue, Susanna Wesley. Her sons, John and Charles Wesley, founded modern Methodism and wrote many of the hymns we still enjoy today. The article read something like, Susanna Wesley was the mother of nineteen children, and yet she still found time to pray. She would take her apron and pull it over her head to signal to others that she needed time with God. No excuses, modern mothers.

Now let's just pause for a moment and think about this. Nineteen. A dozen and a half, plus one more. That's the amount of noisy, messy, hungry humanity that was on the other side of a single sheet of cotton separating Susanna from her army of children. And how much sanctuary did it buy her? Apparently enough that she was still deeply pious. We are meant to conclude that whatever our individual circumstances, nothing should be too much to skip nurturing our spiritual life. Never mind the changes in family roles and methods of child-rearing since then, or the particulars of your life in this moment.

When we are exhausted, it is a difficult thing to bear up under the weight of other people's seeming perfection.

What about when a child is sick, or a partner or parent has dementia? What if there is just not enough? Not enough money or time or energy or help or strength to meet the pressing need. We are barely hanging on, barely holding it together. Rest?! There is no time for rest. You can't imagine adding one more thing to the seven plates you're already spinning.

But here is the truth. You are in this—this chronic unfixable condition called life—and yet at the same time, you are precious beyond rubies. You are worth protecting and preserving. You are meant to be intact.

Jesus said, "I have come that they may have life, and have it to the full" (John 10:10).

Stop and notice. Are you worn out? What do you need? Ask God to show us what leaches the life from our bones. Let us ask God to show us whether there is *anything* we can set down.

Remember, not everything has to be done. And not everything has to be done by you. May you find a small place for rest that is life-giving and fits what is available to you today.

A Blessing for When You're Weary

Oh God, I am so tired. Each breath is shallow. My strength has melted away and hope is hidden behind a wall. I don't even want to crawl out of bed.

I feel alone. The parenting. The endless to-dos. The juggling too much. The spread too thin. Oh God, I cry out to You from the ends of the earth: Show me again how this works—how You bring dry bones to life. Help me.

Blessed are we, the weary and weak and sore, with only the merest ember left burning but who still say: Breathe on me, God. Breathe life into my tired body, my heavy limbs, bring light to the dark corners of my mind. Breathe comfort into my sad heart.

Blessed are we who turn our gaze to seek the One who truly sees us and knows us, like newborns whose bleary sight focuses to find adoring eyes beaming down, delighting and filling, mirroring and multiplying.

Blessed are we who discover we are loved and held in arms that are strong enough to hold that which we cannot.

A GOOD ENOUGH STEP

God built rest into the very architecture of creation. Jesus even took a nap on the bow of a ship in the middle of a storm. If God rests . . . and Jesus rests, certainly we can too. We were never made for boundless energy. Rest reminds us we are human. The world keeps turning, even as we sleep. What brings you rest? Jessica takes baths with extra bubbles. Kate takes a hilariously long, slow walk at the end of each day and tries to leave that day's worries on the path. Carve out time for a nap (even fifteen minutes!). Push snooze one extra time. Go to bed twenty minutes early. Do some small thing that fills your soul.

"Rest—God-centered, Jesus-saturated, Spirit-gifted rest— saved me . . . Rest rescued me from the ruin of restless anxiety." —ADAM MABRY, "Learning How to Rest"

11

HAPPY ENOUGH

My grandpa's favorite place in the world was the Dead Sea. No, not that one. The Dead Sea of Canada. He was a down-home carpenter from the prairies, so the best he could afford was the drive to the western edge of the province of Saskatchewan to Manitou Lake, a mineral spring. In the day he could defy gravity for hours and stretch his legs and arms out on the buoyant surface of the saltwater lake like a human balloon. Then, as the sun set, he could saunter over to the lakefront's dance hall, the fabulously (and appropriately) named Danceland. It was packed seven nights a week, and there my grandpa was able to feel the pull of the full orchestra playing and enjoy another gravity-defying experience: a performance dance floor made in 1928 with horsehair pads placed under a shining maple floor. (Probably the only one left in the world, because, well, that's a strange combo.) But in the middle of nowhere, completely content, he didn't just dance all night long. He *sailed*.

To be honest, that all sounds incredibly fun to me. But if I were to scan a "Top 100 Things to Do Before You Die" list, I doubt that driving to rural Saskatchewan to go swimming in salt and dance on animal hair would appear. Not everyone's dream is Danceland. (I can barely write that word without an exclamation point. *Danceland!*) In fact, our culture has become enamored with a narrow set of criteria about what constitutes a Big Moment. If you're an aspiring social media star in California, you'll need to be photographed in a crown of flowers at Coachella. If you're visiting the Grand Canyon, who but security can pull your spandex body in a yoga pose from teetering on the edge of a cliff? You might be smiling astride a camel in front of the pyramids or throwing yourself out of a plane with a strong series of #skydiving #letgo #limitless hashtags. You did it! You won Instagram!

Desire can feel like an endless hunger, but there is a feeling we get when we feel full: contentment. And it's much harder to describe or explain.

It's difficult to photograph the feeling you get looking out your window or the rush of satisfaction when you see a smiling face. Maybe you want to cherish the perfect cup of tea or get that amazing stretch after actually sleeping through a night. Most of the Big Moments will not seem terribly important to anyone else. They might even feel sort of awful at the time.

The Apostle Paul, sitting in prison, had something rather shocking to say about being content. His friends in Philippi sent him some gifts as he waited behind bars. But Paul made a point of letting them know that with or without their presents, hungry or full, in prison or free, in wealth or poverty, his contentedness remained. This helps to put the popular verse "I can do all things through Christ who strengthens me" (Philippians 4:13) in context. Paul isn't saying he can move mountains or vanquish pain, but that he can find a kind of peace no matter the condition—good or bad—because of Christ's strength. Put in that light, it's not heroic at all. It's more like settling into the moment. Paul learned to be content, but it had nothing to do with his self-sufficiency, sheer luck, satiation, or comfort. He couldn't have known if he would ever be free or how the story would turn out in the end. Rather, his contentment came from God's presence alone.

All of us live inside of an economy of desire. Frankly, who doesn't want to go to Danceland? And there will be times that feel like an endless desert, and times where we get to bob in the lake thinking about lunch. But the freedom is in knowing that, when it comes to desire, you don't have to free-fall to the very bottom. If everything falls apart, you might, like the Apostle Paul, feel something else entirely: contentment. You might feel strangely, weirdly okay.

Sometimes we get to go to the Dead Sea. Other times we are only in rural Saskatchewan. But the best life is the one *we can actually have,* where God promises that, even if there's very little to go around, there will still be Big Moments that feel like enough.

When my mom went back to visit the place her dad had spent his carefree days, she had her own version of Danceland. She wanted to see the local tiny Anglican church, which boasted a medieval stained glass window. After a long search for the key at the locked church (which, it turns out, could be picked up by absolutely anybody at the local RadioShack if you ask for Irene), she popped in to see what was advertised as a stunning historical masterpiece. It wasn't. It was not a miracle window that somehow survived for over five hundred years and was shipped to the New World. It was a very pretty, medium-old window. And my mom was pleased as punch anyway because, hey, it was good enough.

A Blessing for the Life You Have

Blessed are you who hold hope with an open hand.
You who try not to fix your gaze on time's far horizon
or get drunk on what might yet be. And blessed are you
who avoid walking too far down memory lane, getting
stuck wondering if that was as good as it gets, if you've
peaked, or feeling resentful about all that has
disappointed before.

Blessed are you who know that sometimes you need to
stay right here. At least for a minute. Blessed are you
who look wide-eyed, maybe timidly, at the present
moment, gazing at those things that are gently, actually
within the reach of your fingertips.

Blessed are you amid the ordinary details that define
what life is for you, right now. And as you see them,
greet them—each one—as you smile and call them by
name. Everyday joys. Small pleasures. Birds chirping.
Cat cuddles. A cold glass of water. A little child calling
your name. The breeze on your cheeks. The ocean
rhythm. The perfect pillow. The kindness of a friend.
Loves that are and were and ever will be.

May they seem even lovelier, even more delicious
because they become gifts offered anew. May gratitude
fill you, reaching all of the spaces within you that

disappointment left behind and fear has gripped. May something rise in your heart that feels like a strange new kind of contentment.

Because this isn't what you had planned, but it surprises you that even here it can be good. Satisfying. In a way that you know you can come back to. A place that can sustain you through whatever may come.

Blessed are you, finding that life is good because it is enough.

A GOOD ENOUGH STEP

We can be convinced that our happier life, our better self is out there, somewhere. But maybe it's not as out of reach as we thought. Look around. Hold your hand to your chest and feel your steady pulse. What feels like contentment right now? Maybe it is on a dance floor made of horsehair. Or under the stained glass windows of your favorite church. Or right here, at your desk, in your love-worn chair, sitting on the porch listening to the birds. Is it in the warm cup of coffee or the pet curled up at your feet? Whisper a prayer of gratitude for the best of life right now.

"To be grateful is to recognize the Love of God in everything He has given us—and He has given us everything. Every breath we draw is a gift of His love, every moment of existence is a grace, for it brings with it immense graces from Him. Gratitude therefore takes nothing for granted, is never unresponsive, is constantly awakening to new wonder and to praise of the goodness of God. For the grateful person knows that God is good, not by hearsay but by experience. And that is what makes all the difference."

—THOMAS MERTON, *Thoughts in Solitude*

12

RIGHT AFTER IT'S OVER

On a long hike through an Indiana forest, I stumbled upon a spindly tree that had tumbled off a cliff. Walking in the cool caverns below, I could see how the wind and the rain had eroded the ground under its tangled roots. But the tree did not simply fall. It snapped at the base, and tipped over into the chasm beneath. Much to the dismay of my family (who wanted to keep hiking), I was transfixed. The tree didn't die. Or, as I announced loudly to my six-year-old, THE TREE MADE A SERIES OF IMPORTANT CHOICES.

At first the tree grew straight down, as if surrendering to gravity. After all, there was nowhere else to go. But at the point of breaking, the remnant began to thicken. It must have taken years, but its roots grew wider and deeper. Then, in a shocking act of hubris, the tree decided to try growing sideways. It added a few wobbly branches that stuck out utterly horizontally, like a gymnast's arms on a balance beam. More years passed. But at some point, the tree decided that sunlight was a good idea, and the only direction to go was up.

"This is what happens when you anthropomorphize trees," I said, shaking my head. But nonetheless, my eyes got misty as I traced how the trunk made a perfect

U shape and, rather impertinently, grew straight toward the sky.

Can you picture it?

Perhaps you know what it's like to be pushed off the edge. By some gust of wind, you suddenly know your precious lives are hanging on by so little. The human condition is all thin roots and rocky soil, and so you fall.

When your life is snapped at the stem, there is almost nothing to do but watch yourself break. You find yourself trying to remember to breathe. You can hear your own voice, and it might sound strange. Time is slow and surreal. *Is this me? Is this really my life?*

In the aftermath of devastation, the best we can do is survive. Try to sleep. Remember to eat. Keep breathing. Nothing will feel possible, but there you are. Another day. Even that may feel like a miracle.

There comes a season when you begin to realize: *I could stay like this forever*. Overwhelmed and broken. WHO COULD BLAME ME? Did you even hear what happened? It's unthinkable. The world I loved is over now.

Our self-help culture will try to explain to you that this is the time to become better than before. Get back up! There are no setbacks, only setups! This is teaching you something or showing you a different path. Doors are closing and windows are opening, after all. You know, now that we're talking about it, you might even be *lucky* that this happened. After all, this is an opportunity.

The deep evil inherent in the Perfectibility Paradigm is on full display. Your humanity is now a liability. Your grief and fear and confusion and fatigue are wielded as evidence of your failure. You are not only a person who has lost, but a loser.

Please, please, please, hear me say to you: You are not ruined or broken or a failure. You are simply in pain. And God is with you. This is God's great magic act, in my opinion. The more we suffer, the more we can't get away from God's insistent love.

When life is hanging upside down, we must try to send all available energy to the roots. Drink a glass of water. Utter the words "God, help me." Try to get outside. Tell someone that you're struggling. Don't forget to sleep. It might not feel like much. But with these small acts of nurture and taking stock, you are like my favorite tree. You are letting yourself grow straight down.

Grief is a long story.

Someday you might try to get your balance, stretching your branches out a little. Seeing if you can reach and stay stable at the same time. Perhaps a short trip. A more casual conversation with others. Letting your guard down.

There will be days when you will be able to look around and ask: What is here? Where is there some ground to stand on? Is there anything that tastes good now? That nourishes? Where is there room to grow? If so, you might be ready for a turn.

As my friend Nora McInerny says, there is no "moving on." There is only "moving forward." Yes, there will be days when it might be crucial to pull down the blinds and lie in the dark. (Or morally recommit to watching every episode of our favorite television shows, *Community* or *The West Wing*.)

But in the meantime, my dear, you are growing. You are tired and might be scared, and you may have lost too much. But you are not finished yet. Not today.

A Blessing in the Wake of Loss, at the Beginning of Something New

Blessed are you, after the fall. In this new and unrecognizable landscape. At the still point between what was and what's to come. Time has stretched itself, and there seems to be a future somewhere, but it touches you only lightly.

Blessed are you, right here, in between. At the end that comes before the beginning. Knowing that grief is a long story, and maybe, somehow, you are still in it. Growing straight down in the dark where sorrow breathes best. Where roots find their secret springs in crevices that are well hidden. Where God's great magic act of love begins.

Blessed are you, starting to sense that maybe sunlight can reach you, even here. And you reach out, finding yourself in a fierce embrace. And God's voice saying: You are not the bad thing. You are not ruined. You are not broken, nor over, nor a failure, nor learning a lesson. You are my suffering one, and you are loved, you are loved, you are loved.

Blessed are you, maybe ready for the turn. Straight up.

A GOOD ENOUGH STEP

There is something freeing about the in-between. And terrifying. That's when a different kind of prayer works best, one that prays itself.

Just turn your attention to God, and let the prayer be just that. The turning. It's an ancient practice that sounds so spiritual, but it's simple. Center yourself in the desire to pay attention to God and to yourself as God's very own. Set the timer for twenty minutes, and when you find your thoughts wandering to what's for lunch, thank God for the reminder and turn your mind back to prayer that is utterly open, receptive, and soaked in the awareness that God is God. This is getting back to ground, where we know in our bones that we didn't make ourselves.

"Make the most of your regrets; never smother your sorrow, but tend and cherish it till it comes to have a separate and integral interest. To regret deeply is to live afresh."

—HENRY DAVID THOREAU, *The Heart of Thoreau's Journals*

13

NEEDING RULES AT ALL

We crave rules to follow. And, historically, that makes sense. Civilizations and societies are hemmed in by laws like the Ten Commandments, the Noble Eightfold Path, the Beatitudes, the Benedictine Rule, the Five Pillars of Islam, and the Tao.

Even creative practices like art have their own sets of rules. "Art breathes from containments and suffocates from freedom," said Leonardo da Vinci, who knew human eyes are delighted by works that follow rules of proportion, color, and perspective. We generally take more pleasure in poetry that has form—rhyme, meter, stanzas—than we do when we read a poem by an author who ignores accepted conventions. As Robert Frost said, "Writing free verse is like playing tennis without a net." We would get no fun out of playing hide-and-seek if our opponent decided he could use a bloodhound. A chess match in which the pieces could move any number of spaces in any direction would soon be meaningless.

Part of what is so strange about rules is that we love them and hate them at the same time. Let's say we want to become the kind of person or family who treasures what is most important and spends quality time together. Wonderful. Now try discussing how this will have an impact on "screen time" with a teenager and not come away looking like Mussolini.

Freedom and constraint. We hunger for both.

A life of faith must have room for both.

Sometimes reading church history can be very intimidating because everyone important seems to have had *very dramatic instances of holiness*. But let's focus on the little things. Martin Luther, whose actions sparked the Protestant Reformation, recommended a very manageable start to the day. He wrote: "In the morning when you get up, make the sign of the holy cross and say: In the name of the Father and of the Son and of the Holy Spirit. Amen." Not bad. Then he suggests repeating the Apostles' Creed and the Lord's Prayer, but let's not get too fancy here.

It is hard to focus just on the practice itself, not on everything else we pile on top of it. At least that's what comedian Brad Isaac learned when he met a comedy legend. In an interview with Lifehacker, he described bumping into the incomparable Jerry Seinfeld backstage at a club and asking him if he had any advice. Seinfeld suggested that the young comic buy a massive calendar and hang it on the wall. Write a joke every day. Then mark that day with a red X on the calendar.

"After a few days you'll have a chain. Just keep at it and the chain will grow longer every day. You'll like seeing that chain, especially when you get a few weeks under your belt. Your only job is to not break the chain."

Martin Luther and Jerry Seinfeld would probably agree. Don't worry about *everything*. Focus on the small. Start tiny. And keep it up. Try not to break the chain. But if you do, just blink. And start a new one.

A Prayer for This Time of Change

————————

God, I place myself into Your hands. Show me what to do to find the moment of faith I need most—one that will set good things in motion. And establish it in me as a bridge to the next small practice, and the next. Build me up, Lord, that my daily life might be joyful for me and for those around me. Forgive my little (often very fun) rebellions that deceive me into thinking they're for my good. And protect me in this tender time of change. God have mercy. Christ have mercy. Spirit have mercy. *Amen.*

A GOOD ENOUGH STEP

To begin any new practice, we will need to be reminded. Let's find a reminder that works for you. The most effective ones happen every day. Brushing your teeth. Your first sip of coffee. When you plug your phone into the charger before bed. Getting into your car. Filling the dishwasher. Opening your laptop. Jessica changed the name of her morning alarm so every time it rings, it reads: "Rise. Shine. Give God the Glory." Which not only gets a song stuck in your head, if you too grew up in Evangelicalism, but helps to orient the day.

Pick one reminder that you can create an association with. This is your spiritual cue. Then you don't have to worry that you will always drift. You've got a little reminder every day. When it happens, perhaps start small by saying something like "God, today is Yours." Notice how this regular practice helps shape your day.

"Moral excellence comes about as a result of habit. We become just by doing just acts, temperate by doing temperate acts, brave by doing brave acts."

—ARISTOTLE, *Nicomachean Ethics*

14

FOR THE EXILES

There is a saint for almost everything. Fishermen. Hairdressers. Carpenters. Ecologists. Schoolgirls. Lost articles. Housewives. And an obscure Italian teenager who stands in for all those who feel excluded.

Saint Rose was born in thirteenth-century Italy and her astonishing career as a saint began at age three when she raised her aunt from the dead. When I was three, my parents were still calling me "the Bean Bag" because I mostly sat in the middle of the living room. I like to think I was resting up for everything I might try later.

By age seven, Saint Rose decided to live an ascetic lifestyle—taking a vow of poverty, chastity, and obedience—in her parents' house (which I can't imagine looking at my own six-year-old child, who is playing Minecraft as we speak). But she was, by all accounts, a remarkable child. By the age of ten, she had almost died, been miraculously cured, and believed that she'd been empowered by the Virgin Mary to preach on the streets and public squares with a crucifix in her hand. She earned a fearsome reputation as a prophet, and—this I love—someone who could communicate with birds.

But the part of the story that rings through the ages is that she was desperate to join a religious order called the Poor Clares which, ironically, she was too poor to enter. She was expected to pay for entrance with her dowry, and she had none. She loudly prophesied that the religious order who refused her would regret it after her death, which they did only a few short years later. She died at seventeen.

She's now the patron saint of her hometown, Viterbo, Italy, and every year, that town has a procession that honors her and the memory of people who don't fit in. She's known as the saint of exiles. Wanderers. Those refused hospitality by religious communities.

Part of our identities as people of faith is found in community. We are not islands, but reliant on one another to remake us, pull us toward God, and be a soft place to land. As Christians, we believe we are part of the larger body of Christ, through which God unleashes the kingdom. But . . . we are not always wanted.

Our sexual identities leave us locked out. The divorce shatters our family. A compromised immune system means we are less able to join in on Sunday mornings. Mental illness keeps us in bed or a move for work pulls us away. Someone in our family is incarcerated. Our disabilities—or those of our children—cannot or will not be accommodated.

There is a woman at Jessica's church who, at seventeen, found out she was pregnant. She decided to keep her baby, but the decision meant she was an outsider. She didn't fit in with her school friends anymore, and the local moms' group was not a welcoming place for her either. The moms used the weekly gathering as a playdate and to gab about growth charts, humblebrag about which Montessori they got into, and complain about husbands who wouldn't change diapers.

Meanwhile, she was trying to figure out if she could afford formula and how to finish high school with a newborn. She needed help learning how to parent a child, as a child. Plus, she couldn't afford the fee to join the moms' group anyway.

She raised her beautiful daughter mostly on her own.

Then, at twenty-seven, she realized she wanted to make a space for teenage moms so they wouldn't feel so alone. She launched a nonconventional moms' group at church that now serves people in between traditional definitions—teen moms, adoptive moms, foster moms, single moms. They offer practical tips: how to change a diaper, how to advocate for yourself in a hospital, and how to apply for financial assistance. The group has grown to thirty-two parents who are paired with mentor moms who walk them through pregnancy, labor, and infancy. The place that once made her feel like an outsider has now become a welcome mat to other moms like her.

So on the days when you're feeling particularly left out or forgotten, excluded or exiled, let's remember the prophecy of Saint Rose: "You will miss me." We can take a moment to grieve the loss of not being welcomed and remember that all of the community of faith is impoverished when our gifts and our hopes are sent into exile.

Just because we are not always wanted doesn't mean we don't belong.

Also, if you can communicate with birds, please let me know. I have some questions about what a certain owl is saying.

A Prayer for When You Don't Belong

───────────

Dear God,

I always feel like the last one picked. The left out, the unclaimed. It's hard to miss. The face that falls at my presence, the eyes that pretend to not notice, the back turned, or the door that just doesn't open. Those are just the subtle signs. Then there's the name-calling, the abuse, and sometimes even violence. My gifts are not welcome. My tears are not seen. My pain is not registered. I feel invisible.

Oh Jesus, when You walked among us, You became the one rejected. You were abandoned—even betrayed—by Your best friends, barred from the religious institution, rejected by Your very own people. You became one with suffering itself, and as an outcast You opened the door for us to find a home with You, a community of outsiders.

You showed us exactly what You thought of such exclusion and rejection. You loved what the world devalued and demeaned: "the poor, the sick, foreigners, women, those deemed unclean, the imprisoned." You flipped the "who's in" and "who's out" upside down. You radically broke every social and religious barrier—shattering them for all time. Your touch brought healing and restoration and hope to people who too felt like they didn't belong. But You didn't just bring them into the fold. You moved the center of Your kingdom there—with us, the left out. You tell us we belong and call us Your own.

So, blessed are we then who have been excluded, shunned, or forgotten, for there is One who knows us and loves us and walks among us. We know that we are not alone. Our God delights to be with us, and has moved heaven and earth just to be where we are. Blessed are we who belong here, with God, and who make space for others to sit with us, who practice radical belonging and hospitality because we know what it is like to be locked out.

Amen.

A GOOD ENOUGH STEP

Finding a prayer practice that engages you can take time and may involve trying a bunch of new ideas. I (Jessica) find that sometimes simply setting a time to pray doesn't help center my attention. I can as easily get distracted by the dog or the laundry or my grumbling stomach. Practices that give me a bit more structure help to direct me to my deepest hope, deepest need, deepest longing.

Today, write a prayer in the form of a haiku. A haiku is a Japanese poem that has three lines, each with a set number of syllables: 5-7-5. No need to rhyme, but notice how the structure helps focus your attention and conversation with God.

Here's an example:

God is in all things.
Let light speak through the moment.
The wait is over.

"Happiness is not only a hope, but also in some strange manner a memory . . . we are all kings in exile."

—G. K. CHESTERTON, *The Thing: Why I Am a Catholic*

15

THE TRAGEDY OLYMPICS

The aerial shots of the Tuscan countryside and the slopes of Machu Picchu glide across the screen as a row of manicured and glossy twenty- and thirty-somethings croon-shriek their greetings. All is love and loveliness in the universe of the television show called *Bachelor in Paradise*.

The tragic drama immediately presents. The girls aren't getting along! The bachelor and bachelorettes already have favorites! A contestant's old flame shows up and tries to take back his girl—a move one contestant calls "the tragedy of his life."

Say what you want about reality TV, but this series brings us unadulterated, un-cerebral joy. But we liked it a little better before we started tallying how often the contestants use the word *tragedy* to describe their hair . . . wardrobe malfunctions . . . accidentally ordering a virgin daiquiri . . . not receiving the rose . . . having second thoughts. You know, not really tragic stuff?

When life gives you a monthly subscription to miserable news, it's really hard to take other people's problems seriously. Especially when we all know that person who overplays their hand. Store was out of their favorite La Croix flavor? *Tragedy!* They missed the new episode of *House Hunters*? *How will they live!* Kid refused to wear the larger-than-their-face bow you picked out for picture day? *Quelle horreur!*

Tragedies are life-altering events. Not mere inconveniences. So when pop culture overuses the word *tragedy,* it makes me want to whip out my metaphorical hard-times-pin-collection like a jaded Girl Scout with the heaviest sash.

Going through something terrible can make you want to become the "perspective police," to command everyone to shut their pieholes until they *fully recognize* how horrible things are for you. Life can quickly become a measuring stick of suffering. Hard day at the office? *That sucks, but are your organs literally eating themselves alive?*

I used to find myself looking at people and muttering, *"You're fine."* But one ordinary day, I had a good scan. Immediately after, I got in the Duke University Hospital elevator with a really nice older man who was coming from the brain cancer area with his hospital bracelet on, obviously processing some tough news, and I lost it. Tears streamed down my face; it all came flooding back: the realization that life is hard, and it's hard for everyone.

So maybe cut your very irritable neighbor some slack if they are muttering under their breath *again.* Or that Facebook friend who only posts photos of their minor ankle injuries for pity. Or the colleague who insists on googling another symptom on WebMD. When people enter the Tragedy Olympics, they don't always realize that it's not actually a game. It's just life, and we are all, for better or worse, players who need each other more than we need an award.

A Blessing for When You Realize Everyone Is Struggling

Blessed are you who have realized that life is hard. And it's hard for everyone. Your awareness came at a cost. You lost something you can't get back. You were diagnosed with chronic pain or degenerative disease. Your family fell apart and things have never been the same.

Blessed are you who gave up the myth that the good life is one of happiness, success, perfection. The life that looks beautiful on Facebook, but isn't real. You who realize it is okay to not be okay. To not have a shiny life, because no one does.

Blessed are you who see things clearly, where struggle is everyone's normal. You walk among the fellowship of the afflicted, a club no one wants to join. And while this life isn't shiny, it does come with superpowers. Superpowers of ever-widening empathy and existential courage that get you back up after another fall and a deepened awe at the beauty and love that can be found amid life's rubble. Like flowers that grow from the cracks in the sidewalk. These virtues blossom in you. And thank God for you.

Blessed are all of us who struggle, for we are in good company, and we'll never walk alone.

A GOOD ENOUGH STEP

Sometimes, when I'm frustrated and don't know what to *do* to make myself feel better . . . be kinder . . . have more patience . . . or handle the colleague who continues to complain about her *very* small problem, I center myself by practicing breath prayer. These are tiny prayers that remind us that God is as near as our breath, and sometimes the act of breathing in and of itself can be prayer. Try it.

1. On a long inhale, hold these words in your mind: *Giver of all life.*
2. Then, on a long exhale, hold these words: *Give me patience to face today.*
3. Repeat for three long, deep breaths.

Urban Dictionary, a website that keeps close track of everyday speech, defines the phrase "The Suffering Olympics" as "the pointless endeavor of comparing different tragedies or histories of oppression to one another by attempting to quantify the suffering and/or injustice of each, so as to determine which tragedy was more tragic, or which oppressed peoples were more unjustly oppressed." When we have experienced loss, or pain, or disease, we are often tempted to play this game too. On hearing of someone else's distress, we might find ourselves saying, "You think that's bad? Last Christmas, I had a goiter so swollen that . . ."

We all want our troubles to mean something, to have stature and be validated—but we gain nothing by pitting our woes against another's. Pain should unite us, as fellow sufferers, as fellow humans. Regardless of who feels worse, we need each other.

16

THE BAD THING

There's that part of the conversation when you start apologizing.

"Thanks so much for listening for so long . . ."

"Sorry . . . I know this is a lot. . . ."

"I shouldn't be telling you all this. It's so depressing."

You needed someone to listen, sit close as the story unspools. *I didn't want my life to be this way. I don't know how I'm going to move forward. I'm so scared.*

What's been happening to you is *awful*. It's unbearable. You wanted to share it with someone else, but there's a moment when it starts to feel like it may be too much. *Does anyone else really want to hear this? Maybe this is too much. Maybe I'm too much.* The pain of the experience is now transforming into something else: embarrassment, sadness, a new wave of loneliness.

Last night, I was sitting on the couch with one of my best friends who is terribly sick. After a sudden cancer diagnosis, she is struggling through treatment that leaves her too thin, sallow, and struggling to get out of bed. She has lost all her thick, mermaid hair, and her small head is covered in a patchy fuzz. She is powering through with all her tiny might, but this disease does not care how hard she tries.

She tries to change the subject, not for her, but for

me. Cancer is a living death, and she wants to spare me. I can see it in her giant eyes ("You have Disney eyes," I always tell her). She is starting to believe that it's too much. She is too much. She is "the Bad Thing."

There is tremendous pressure in our positive-thinking society to avoid sad stories. Think positively! Speak positively! Reframe and look on the bright side! But unfortunately for Christians, we are handed a deeply sad story. Our God came to earth and took on full humanity just long enough to be murdered. Jesus rose from the grave and death was conquered, but most of Jesus's closest friends and disciples followed him to early graves. The New Testament is brimming with courage and holiness because the early church understood that faith was not a pleasant guarantee. Our faith is the promise that we will learn something about a great mystery, how we can be loved and saved and changed by a God who shows us what it means to be human. It is beautiful and terrible, but it is not "positive." At least not the way our culture imagines.

After seeing my friend, I cried all the way home in the car. Because of her pain. Because it is costing her everything. Because we live in a world where people are sick or betrayed or lonely or scared. I cried because *this is life*.

But a truth bubbled up in the midst of it: I felt more than sad. I felt love, fear, and awe.

Seeing pain up close can give you an incredible experience of awe. It's like seeing a garment turned inside out and all the rough seams are showing. You see someone's absolute humanity shine through all the pain, and that vulnerability makes them more—not less—beloved.

We feel it when we see a baby being born, or when holding someone's hand as he passes from this life. The great mystery of the world is peeking through, and we get just a glimpse. The German philosopher and theologian Rudolf Otto called it "the numinous." We understand holiness and mystery and fear and humility all in the same moment. And it is beautiful.

I wish I had known that when I was in pain, when I truly believed that I was "the Bad Thing." But people's pain is not only a burden. It is an opportunity to scoot up close to the deepest parts of who we are and what comprises our humanity.

Our positive-thinking world might miss it, but our faith allows us to see that pain is not simply a sad story. There is nothing inherently embarrassing or shameful about it.

We are not the bad thing. We are simply living our beautiful, terrible days.

A Blessing for When You Feel Like the Bad Thing

Blessed are you who feel like the bad thing. You are everyone's reminder of their frailty, of life's cruelty. Your chronic pain or depression or regular scans remind those around you that life isn't as fair or easy as they had hoped.

Blessed are you who try to hide your humanity. You who temper your complaints, who avoid mentioning your next appointment, who pretend you are doing better than you are to make reality a little more palatable for others. You, who try and try and try to make yourself easier to love, easier to be around, easier to manage.

But, dear one, *blessed are you* because you are not the bad thing. Your illness or grief or despair or addiction is not too much. It's just your humanity showing.

And *blessed are we* who get to see it up close. Who, despite our own fears and reminders of our finitude, get to hold your hand as you face each day with courage, confronting things you didn't choose. It is this kind of courageous living—the kind that shows all the shabby edges—that we are so thankful to witness. You, blessed one, remind us that life is so beautiful and life is so hard. And we feel lucky for the privilege to do life with you—no matter how difficult, no matter how messy. You are not the bad thing. You are a gift. And we love every bit of you.

A GOOD ENOUGH STEP

Think of someone you know right now who struggles with a chronic illness or an autoimmune disease like fibromyalgia or lupus or another thing that you can't spell, let alone pronounce. Someone who lost a spouse or a baby. Someone who is in the throes of depression or caregiving for an aging parent. Someone who has struggled with addiction or disordered eating. People who know long-suffering and who endure the not-easily-overcomeable. How can you practically remind them that they are not the bad thing? Can you write them a note of encouragement? Spend time in prayer for them? Offer to do something concrete—pick up groceries, mow their lawn, buy them a gift card? Do something that will remind them they are not alone. That they are seen and loved even in the midst of the struggle.

"Those that lack friends to open themselves unto are cannibals of their own hearts. But one thing is most admirable . . . which is, that this communicating of a man's self to his friend works two contrary effects; for it redoubleth joys, and cutteth griefs in halves. For there is no man that imparteth his joys to his friend, but he joyeth the more; and no man that imparteth his griefs to his friend, but he grieveth the less." —FRANCIS BACON, "Of Friendship"

17

HOPPING OFF THE TREADMILL

One of the great French indictments of the North American culture of work goes something like this: *Americans live to work. The French work to live.*

I find that to be wonderfully damning, because there is nothing I relate to more than the desire to make busyness a balm for our frenetic lives.

There is a sobering connection, however, between activity and the nature of work itself that we can discover from a nineteenth-century experiment in punishment.

In 1818, a civil engineer named William Cubitt put his mind to addressing a perplexing social problem. Prisons, it seemed, were not places for deterring criminal activity, but for refining it. Younger offenders mixed with the more experienced and emerged from prison better skilled, and more embedded in criminal ways. It occurred to Cubitt that he had skills that could put prisoners to work in ways that could train them in useful labor, curb social interaction, and better prepare them for life beyond prison. The son of a miller, he invented the "treadwheel," or treadmill—a massive paddle wheel set beside a platform where prisoners could be positioned to step on an endless staircase that rose up before them as the wheel turned. Sometimes the wheel they turned ground corn or pumped water, but in many prisons the treadmill did nothing but keep the men walking for six to ten hours a day. They milled air.

Social interaction among the men on the treadmill was curbed by the building of partitions between them. Loneliness and monotony became the most dreaded aspect of the treadmill. And the public was invited to watch, and allowed to jeer and taunt the prisoners laboring on the wheel. Oscar Wilde was one who served time on the prison treadmill. Its use was discontinued by the turn of the century, when society deemed it a form of torture to set men to work that had no meaning and allowed no human connection.

Today, the treadmill metaphor has a similar connotation. When we say we want to "get off the treadmill," we are saying we want lives that are meaningful. We feel trapped in activities that are monotonous and carry little meaning or purpose. We might feel we are climbing an "endless staircase" of achievement, for high grades or success. Like an M. C. Escher drawing, we might feel caught in an endless staircase of caregiving, work, or social pressure.

In such situations, we long to stop and get off the endless round of meaningless activity with unending loneliness. Life reduced to buttoning and unbuttoning. Punching in and punching out. Heating up more chicken nuggets. Did I just hear the laundry wash cycle finish?

What is it that is driving us, chasing us, propelling us to continue this unstoppable effort? What are we trying to reach or achieve?

And what would it take to just stop?

A shift in responsibilities? A lower set of expectations? Or self-permission? A change of perspective?

It's okay to get off the treadmill of meaningless work, even one that was productive for you at one time in your life. Even a daily practice of prayer that is life-giving can lose its meaning if it becomes a treadmill.

Most of us are turning the wheel of obligation in our lives. People depend on us. Nothing ever stops. Regardless, we need a sober look at reality to stop pretending that there is unlimited energy or endless time to do what is meaningful. To attend to the values we cherish most. And stop the mindless pressures that we have placed on ourselves.

Seriously. If we stopped, would we fall off?

As Martin Luther said to Philip Melanchthon, "Philip, let's go fishing. Today we can leave the governance of the universe to God."

A Blessing for Slowing Down

Blessed are we who thought we were self-made by the doing, by the accolades, by the accomplishments, and by the gold stars. We measured our worth by how tired we were every morning, how many special events we missed because of work, by how many times we answered "How are you?" with "Busy." We thought: *This is the good life.*

But then we grew tired and lonely. We felt the strain on our relationships and our spiritual lives. And we became a bit miserable to be around.

So *blessed are we* who stop—okay, maybe not stop entirely, who are we kidding—but who slow down. We who discover rest and new life and renewal when we step off the treadmill (or at least turn it down). We who remember that the world keeps spinning without us. And thank God for that. We who remember that we are loved, loved, loved. Not for what we do, but for who we are.

A GOOD ENOUGH STEP

Take a moment to be curious. What are the nonnegotiables of your day? The bare essentials?

Saying "I love you" to your spouse or child. Getting outside. Being creative. Slowing down. Doing that one boring thing that you have been avoiding. Being frivolous. Practicing the daily office. Calling your dad. Playing with your grandkid.

You might be a workaholic or a champion avoider, but here's a chance to step off the treadmill—the myth of hyper-productivity or of bottomless energy or need-to-say-yes-to-every-request-that-comes-your-way may not be serving you like you once thought.

Of course, we can't stop everything. But maybe we can take off the burdens we've self-imposed. Knowing, trusting that you are loved just as you are. No amount of doing will change that.

"Who's chasing you?!"

—Someone yelling at one of the authors while she was describing her workday

18

HELLO, GOODBYE

A life is made up of so many beginnings and so many endings.

We start new jobs and we leave old ones. We move to new cities and leave our childhood hobbies in our parents' basements. We become new people, slowly. Friends and relationships come and go. Hopes appear, and then they fade away.

If you are under the lovely illusion that you haven't changed, pull out an old diary or clean a messy closet. What's that? You once devoted your life to scrapbooking every memory with a custom laser printer? You used to run cross-country? We are different, and so are the people we loved. Try writing down the names of your closest friends from five, ten, and twenty years ago. Who were we, and *why didn't anyone tell us to stop massacring our eyebrows?*

The strangest part of change, I suppose, is how it occurs as a series of small funerals. We lay our dreams to rest. *Goodbye, love.* You lit up my world. *Goodbye, job.* You were the mold that I poured myself into. *Goodbye, self.* I need to let go now, and I can hardly begin to try.

A friend is changing jobs and she finds herself crying over a small thank-you email from a colleague. *I hope this work mattered. But if I had been treated better, could I have stayed?* Another has discovered that her marriage is ending and there's nothing she can do. *I'm not trying to be melodramatic, but I barely get out of bed.* They are stuck trying to account for two simultaneous truths: 1) a world I loved is ending, and 2) it happens every day.

I have many delightful friends who try to solve the sorrow inherent in change by giving it up entirely. Routines become a bulwark against the threat of pain. They brush their teeth at dawn. They watch *Jeopardy!* right before dinner, and there had better be an encroaching hurricane if you're calling them on the phone. They vacation in the same spot and they have some very unchristian feelings about people who sit in their pew or take their treadmill at the gym. (Okay, that is everyone.)

But suffering, explained the author C. S. Lewis, is the order of nature. Avoid it and you will find that you've squeezed out life itself.

Six months ago, a good friend discovered that her partner was unfaithful and that their marriage was over. Her son would have to say goodbye to spaghetti dinners, road trip harmonizing, and his bedroom with his stickers on the door. She would be leaving behind a high school romance, a decade of friendship, the smell of his salty skin at the beach and immeasurably more. As a new mother-and-son duo, they would have to say hello to a new life, school district, friends, habits, and the courage to climb a ladder to clean the eaves of an aging new home in the spring.

When I spoke to her recently, I noticed that the unthinkable had happened: everything had changed. She had learned how to do basic plumbing. She even had a date scheduled for Friday. And she still cries when she makes spaghetti because family dinner is not what it was supposed to be.

Her approach to change mirrors much of what Stanford psychologist Carol Dweck describes in her now classic work, *Mindset: The New Psychology of Success,* comparing a "fixed" versus "growth" mindset. A fixed mindset assumes that whatever we are—a certain composite of personality, intelligence, abilities—is a given. Every new challenge becomes a moment where you simply prove yourself again and again as being that particular person (dumb, smart, winning, losing, etc.). A growth mindset, conversely, imagines that we are not static creatures. We can change, and we do. We flex and grow, fall back, or bounce forward. But we are not simply the aggregate of whatever we have been.

Not every change is going to be a transformation. But every change can be an opportunity for grace, that divine approval that God doles out regardless. Did we become better or worse? Holier or crustier? Softer or quicker on the draw? God will show up regardless, silently pouring forgiveness and encouragement into our too-open hearts.

A Blessing for Hellos and Goodbyes

Blessed are you on the brink of something new. A new life. A new career. A new commitment. A new relationship. A new decade. Blessed are you, dear one, so full of hope, you whose horizon extends far beyond what your eyes can see. May your celebration be sweet and delicious and perhaps contain some singing. This new thing is worth rejoicing. May the joy that buoys you today carry you through the difficult spots to come.

And blessed are you, closing the door on something you once loved. A home. A dream. A business. A marriage. You who fought and pleaded, tried and prayed. When the weight of the world rests on your shoulders and you feel as though you may drown under paperwork. You who sit in grief and despair, and maybe a little fearful for what happens . . . now.

May you, dear one, find comfort from places and people you don't anticipate who remind you that you are not alone. You may be saying goodbye to something—someone dear . . . but something new will be born. I cannot promise it will replace what was there, and I won't try to tell you it will always be better. But, I do believe that we can find beauty, meaning, and truth right where we stand.

In our transitions. In our hellos and our goodbyes. And yes, even on the other side.

A GOOD ENOUGH STEP

Find a small notepad—a really tiny one. And if you've a mind to, a cup of tea or a glass of wine—maybe a large one. This is the place where goodbyes will happen. And reverent celebrations of what was. Grab an old catalog or magazine, tape, a pair of scissors, and a pen or pencil. Leaf through the pictures, and if anything stirs up a memory that is from the old life, cut it out and tape it in your book, or write a word that best symbolizes that memory. Take your time. Honor it for what it was. And wasn't. You did what you knew to do, for what you knew then. And when you are ready, turn the page.

Again, on a new page, let something come to you that deserves a proper goodbye. With each symbol or image, let the full knowledge of all that it means resonate within you. And let it be what it was. And say to yourself, you did what you knew to do, for what you knew then.

You may want to take breaks. And carry on another time. You'll know when the memories start to settle into a peace.

Then when they do, write down the date and the time, and these words: *I did what I knew to do, with what I knew then.* When we see our decisions and experiences as having a time and date and a context, we can offer ourselves a gentle compassion. And permission to close the book. And let each day give us our new time, to do what we know to do. With what we know now.

"Truth makes love possible; love makes truth bearable."

—ROWAN WILLIAMS, *A Ray of Darkness*

19

NO REASON WHATSOEVER

*O*ur culture says that everything has to be *for* something. Reading is for self-improvement. Hobbies are for enrichment. Didn't you know? Your child's soccer practice is a long-haul attempt to better a college application. Your crappy watercolor painting has to hang in the living room or else that afternoon was a waste. Didn't you know that you're supposed to be getting better all the time?

It's called "hyper-instrumentalization." The obsession with use. It's a symptom of the pragmatism that has wound its way into almost every part of American culture. How useful was your day?

When our lives get overwhelming, it's tempting to begin to use this logic as a weapon against ourselves. Look at us! Failing to multitask! Failing to render all goods into ideas and practices and moments that can be useful.

It might seem counterintuitive, then, that when life is at its worst, I don't turn to doing *nothing*. Naps and television and sitting around are great. But when a week is full of terrible appointments or when I can't seem to get out of an anxious thought loop, I need something to *do* when life feels so out of control.

I remember really vividly this one terrible week where

I went from the medical hellscape to a work trip. It sounds horrible. But I took an approach that taught me a really important lesson. And here it is.

You can find incredible peace and joy when you discover you are doing something for *no reason at all*.

Did I help skin an elk for an indigenous studies class? Yes! I did skin an elk! (Lots of strong shoulder work.)

Did I go visit the World's Largest Ukrainian Sausage? I sure did!

I learned how to make schpritzel-something-or-others because my old college roommate is obsessed with German cookie making. And I watched a soloist hammer out the chords on her guitar in a park like she didn't care if any person on any planet wanted to follow her on Twitter.

I have always said that I don't have hobbies, I have friends. And maybe I don't need to be bird-watching much on the side. But I do need to cultivate a habit that my friends have already figured out: just trying feels so good.

When the stakes are low, you can return to the beautiful stupidity of caring.

My husband plays defense on an intramural hockey league because when he tried out, he was one of the only people who could skate backward. (I wish I could explain to non-Canadians just how funny that is.) But he plays because he likes the way it feels (to rack up penalty minutes).

My friend Will was recently found in his garage using a saw to cut out a wooden snake. Because he decided the house was missing something: wooden snakes.

So maybe *today* you need permission to do something for no reason whatsoever.

Bake the cookies your great aunt used to make . . . even if they don't turn out perfectly. Read a poem out loud with a fake Swedish accent. Lie in the grass and form cloud animals or dream up new constellations. Take a drive to the nearest roadside attraction (and please report back). Take up whittling or learn to cross-stitch an inappropriate saying onto a pillow.

Remember: We're not aiming for perfect. We're just trying to remember to ask ourselves: How does it feel to try?

A Blessing for Finding
Delight in a Difficult Day

———————

Blessed are you when life has handed you yet another serious mess. Instead of turning straight to worry or despair or fear or dread, you set it down for a minute and say, "I'll get to that later. I've got something ridiculous to do. And it's urgent." Blessed are you who do something you've never tried that must be done right now, because failing doesn't matter. You know that it feels so good to try.

Blessed are we, the responsible, who take a nonlinear path. Who, as the poet Wendell Berry says, "every day do something that won't compute." Who know that right when life gets heavy or hard or too much, we must carve a path to delight. Who do something for no reason whatsoever but for joy.

Blessed are you who see the art in absurdity. Because when you think about it, life is unexpectedly and terribly and wonderfully absurd. So why don't we just embrace it?

So, blessed are you when you grow too many tomatoes of more than one variety. Or solve a mystery while playing interactive glow-in-the-dark miniature golf. Or who learn a new dance or create a band out of kitchen instruments or make a cake that looks like the Leaning Tower of Pisa (you only name it such in retrospect). This is only the beginning.

A GOOD ENOUGH STEP

You know it is coming. It's your turn to do something for no reason whatsoever. Like learning another language to find the words that don't exist in English. After all, why is there a word in German that means "a face badly in need of a fist"? Or in Brazilian Portuguese, a tiny word that means "tenderly running your fingers through your lover's hair"? I don't know, but how great is that trivia? Finger-paint with water on the sidewalk. Learn the alphabet backward. Make up new names for all the plants you can see (dandelions are obviously better known as "puff-buzzers"). Pick something, anything, that may seem like a colossal waste of time, but matters simply because it makes you smile.

"Consider the ravens: They do not sow or reap, they have no storeroom or barn; yet God feeds them. And how much more valuable you are than birds! Who of you by worrying can add a single hour to your life? Since you cannot do this very little thing, why do you worry about the rest? Consider how the wildflowers grow. They do not labor or spin. Yet I tell you, not even Solomon in all his splendor was dressed like one of these. If that is how God clothes the grass of the field, which is here today, and tomorrow is thrown into the fire, how much more will he clothe you—you of little faith!" (Luke 12:24–28)

Jesus explains that even the lilies and the grass of the fields are clothed and the birds of the air are cared for, so how much more will God care for you? It's a lovely thought when taken at face value, but we know that birds fall from the sky or fly into windows. Lilies shrivel up. Grass withers and dies. What reassurance might Jesus be offering, then?

It is not our *infiniteness* that Jesus promises, but God's *attentiveness*. No matter what is keeping you up at night or what feels overwhelming, God has not left your side. God sees you. God has not forgotten you. God is awake.

20

BECOMING REAL

We come undone.

It's not a pretty fact, but it is inevitable. There are seasons when we are making and building, growing and transforming into the person we always hoped we'd be. We become the kind of person who does yoga. Or watches every classic movie. Or finally checks our voicemails.

Then we come apart, and all of our rough edges are showing again. And it is in seasons like that when I need to hear the gospel of the Velveteen Rabbit.

The Velveteen Rabbit is a children's book that tells the story of a stuffed toy rabbit wondering what to do when he is replaced by windup toys or eventually cast away. The bunny was once lovely, but now is ragged. Older. Careworn.

Perhaps that is a familiar feeling. We see a photograph of our younger selves—maybe living a life that is now gone—and we have a little pang. *That's me. And she's gone. He's gone.* And we wholeheartedly accept the idea that we were better before. There is a shiny version of ourselves that once existed and, whoever we are now, it can never be as good.

The Velveteen Rabbit has a moment of candor about this fear when talking to the Skin Horse, a toy who is older and wiser than the other toys. And the Skin Horse explains that in the process of being loved, we are not diminished. We are becoming *real*.

Real is not about how you are made, says the horse. It happens *to* you. It might hurt. And it happens slowly, over time. But when you are really, really loved, you become real.

The author of the story, Margery Williams, understood the deep beauty of that kind of love. She had come to love literature through her father, who died suddenly when she was seven. In her stories for children, there is a tender ache for the lives we've lost and the loves that endure. We are changed, and we often wish it were otherwise.

Sometimes we worry that we are being undone, unmade, that we are simply losing our polish. But we are *becoming*. Like a well-worn stuffy that has been dragged everywhere and slept with every night and hugged to tatters, we become real through our wear and tear.

By healing from the cruelty we didn't deserve.

By keeping a soft heart for those who need us.

By being loved imperfectly and loving imperfectly. In both, we changed. And keep changing. We were not kept in a box on a shelf, and it shows.

As the Skin Horse explains, "Generally, by the time you are Real, most of your hair has been loved off, and your eyes drop out and you get loose in the joints and very shabby. But these things don't matter at all, because once you are Real you can't be ugly, except to people who don't understand." Our shabbiness might be unacceptable to an Instagram world. After all, our culture confuses glamour with beauty, and wisdom with bylines.

May we always know the difference.

May we not despise our realness. And when we worry we are coming undone or not as lovely as we were before, may we not be confused. After all, we can never be ugly, except to people who don't understand.

A Blessing for Becoming Real

Blessed are we who are becoming, who have lived so long in this strange state we call time that it shows. We are changing, and that's how we know we are alive.

Blessed are you who see the evidence of your own becoming, the places where you are worn from so much loving. The laugh lines from jokes that made your belly ache. Crow's feet from squinting to see the stars. Stretch marks from growing babies, building muscle, enjoying delicious meals. And yes, the places that hurt. That are visibly still wounded and sore, that change how you move or how you live.

Blessed are you, seeing all this as evidence of loss, yes, but also of life, because what is real is now showing through. Blessed are you who do not despise your realness. It may hurt. You may not recognize yourself in the mirror. But this is what we hoped for, right? To live and love. To be loved. To have our experiences show on our faces and in our cells. It is the real life of Jesus in us, being made visible, as all our seams show.

A GOOD ENOUGH STEP

Find a minute alone. Take out a photo of yourself as a child. Allow yourself to appreciate what was—who you were. All the pain you had yet to know or perhaps already did know. The way your body moved easily, when sleep came effortlessly. The expectations you had. But then also take time to tell your younger self all the ways that living and aging and suffering have carved out within you a space for reality and more love and compassion for others. Be effusive! If a prayer comes, pray it. If a poem appears, write it. If you want to create art, do it.

"Our bloom is gone. We are the fruit thereof."

—WALLACE STEVENS, "Le Monocle de Mon Oncle"

21

#BLESSED

We don't live in a culture of *blessing*. We live in a culture of #Blessed.

Partially nude bikini shot? #Blessed. Christmas card professional photo shoot where everyone is looking directly at the camera wearing matching chambray tops? #Blessed.

As Christians, we cross-stitch our blessings on pillows, hand-letter them in whimsical fonts, and tattoo them on our bodies, forgetting, perhaps, that Jesus turned the idea of what makes us blessed upside down. His blessings should leave some people wide-eyed, and others with tears of relief streaming down their cheeks.

Jesus says, blessed are you when you are at the end of your rope. When you are exhausted and despairing. When tears are your food, morning and night. When your stomach grumbles and your mouth is dry. Blessed are you who forgives the person who never said sorry and who definitely didn't deserve your forgiveness. You who are ridiculed and humiliated, left out and left behind. The timid and the soft-spoken. The one who works toward peace instead of the easy road of vengeance.

So much of how we interpret these blessings depends on where we are sitting when we hear them.

Maybe we are like the respected and applauded religious leaders in Jesus's time. We've elbowed our way to the front row, or perhaps we were ushered in by privilege and birthright. We say and do the right things. Our righteousness is on full display on Instagram. Our chest puffs with pride at how well life has worked out—our beautiful family, our comfortable bank account, our healthy body. These beatitudes should make us uncomfortable. Because God is celebrating who we try so hard *not* to be. *Dependent. Needy. Desperate.*

These blessings will sound quite different if you're the one at the back of the crowd. The one who barely feels like you belong in the first place. The one who's scared someone will find out that you don't have it all together.

Jesus often taught by taking something conceptual and comparing it to something concrete. For example, "The kingdom of heaven is like a treasure hidden in a field" (Matthew 13:44). To his hearers who grew up in farms and fields, this would be tactile, not just intellectual. It's a rhetorical device that doesn't need detailed notes or a tape recorder. You'd remember.

In these blessings, it's like Jesus is pulling examples from the very people listening in. "Blessed are you, Jamie, even when you mourn the person you lost." "Blessed are you, Sarah, though you are struggling to find hope." "Blessed are you, John, when there isn't enough to feed your family."

He was looking into the eyes of those who felt like the misfits. And then used the everyday experiences of weeping, hungering, thirsting, suffering as a badge of belonging.

The left out will be welcomed with a warm embrace. The forgotten will not just be remembered but honored. The ones who don't have it all together are exactly who God is inviting into the kingdom. In fact, the whole kingdom belongs to the ones on the edges. This is the upside-down kingdom—directly available to those of us who don't have it all together.

Sometimes the only thing that's possible is to bless life's every present moment—even, and especially, the hard ones. Blessings in those moments fall like a summer rain over the driest times and places in our lives. And though a blessing seems counterintuitive in moments of grief and sorrow, that's when you need to be reminded of the presence of God most—the God whose kingdom is available to all of us.

The world looks a bit strange from here, upside down. But maybe it's how it's supposed to be: our feet rooted in heaven.

A Blessing for When You Don't Feel #Blessed

Blessed am I when I lose sleep over what troubles me. When my worries keep me watching the clock tick by. When I have no energy to do anything but fret. The kingdom of God is here and now.

Blessed am I when I am drowning in grief. When wave after wave after wave crashes over me. When I start to feel okay, then something reminds me of what I've lost, and I'm pulled under once again. God promises to comfort me.

Blessed am I when I feel silenced and afraid to speak up. When I am forgotten and left out. When I feel small and feel as though my work, my presence, my life doesn't matter. The whole world is mine.

Blessed am I when I am starving for justice. When the world around me feels so unfair that I could scream, but no one seems to be listening. No one seems to care. May justice flow like a river.

Blessed am I when someone hurts me, when I feel offended, and I don't return insult with insult. Instead, I forgive, recognizing the number of times I've needed to be forgiven.

Blessed am I when I strip away all the extra. When I see the world as it really is—broken, tender, fragile, beautiful. These are the same eyes that see God in everything too.

Blessed am I when I take the hard road. The winding one that doesn't opt for the shortcut of rage or resentment or unkind words. That doesn't pave over with trite niceties, but walks toward peacemaking. For I am God's kid.

Blessed am I when I face hardships of all sorts. Insults, hurt feelings, lies, and vindictive neighbors (why is loving your *actual* neighbor so hard, God?). Blessed am I when I work to usher in God's kingdom of love and compassion and justice and forgiveness and peace, even when it's hard.

Blessed are we. The imperfect and don't-have-it-all-together. God's beloved.

A GOOD ENOUGH STEP

"We must bless without wanting to manipulate. Without insisting that everything be straightened out right now. Without insisting that our truth be known. This means simply turning whoever it is we need to bless over to God, knowing that God's powerful love will do what our own feeble love or lack of it won't. I have suggested that it is a good practice to believe in six impossible things every morning before breakfast, like the White Queen in *Through the Looking Glass*. It is also salutary to bless six people I don't much like every morning before breakfast."

—MADELEINE L'ENGLE, *A Stone for a Pillow*

Your turn. Think of six people you don't like very much. I certainly didn't have to look too far. Bless them. Even . . . *especially* . . . if you don't want to.

"The Lord bless you and keep you; the Lord make his face to shine upon you and be gracious to you; the Lord lift up his countenance upon you and give you peace."

(Numbers 6:24–26)

These familiar words are found on the oldest surviving biblical text, engraved on two silver amulets from the seventh century B.C.E. unearthed near Jerusalem. This was the blessing that Moses told Aaron, the high priest, and his sons to give to the people. For over three thousand years it has been intoned in synagogues. The blessing is probably the favorite passage from the Jewish scriptures for Christians. It is a frequent benediction that ends times of worship. It is a threefold blessing that reminds Christians of the Trinity and the injunction of Jesus to bless in the name of the Father, the Son, and the Holy Spirit.

22

LOVING WHAT IS

It drives me a little bananas every time someone says, "The best is yet to come." Yes, there are beautiful promises in scripture that promise that God has set a future before us. The book of Philippians reminds us, after all, that "he who began a good work in you will carry it on to completion until the day of Christ Jesus."

But, if we're honest, we may find ourselves saying: "Sometimes the best is behind me."

Sometimes we have crescendoed. Sometimes we have finished singing the song of our career. Sometimes we have finished humming the tune of our parenthood, either because we didn't have that baby or they are grown and gone. Maybe we are playing the closing notes of the life of a friend, parent, or child. We are singing, knowing that someday the last note will be sung.

After all, there is so much to sing out. Scripture reminds us that we are more splendid than the lilies of the field. The hairs on our head are numbered by God. Combing through the details of our lives, past and present, we could likely pull out a thousand examples of moments to celebrate. Fall leaves. Dulce de leche ice cream. The softness of your grandmother's skin. But we are surrounded by reminders of experiences that have come and gone. New parenthood. That past love. The first day of school. It is over now.

Is it okay to acknowledge what's behind us? And can we still love what is ahead?

When we start to have more past than future, we must allow ourselves a gentle honesty. Just as God numbers the hairs on our head, so too our days on earth can be counted. This ends, and part of accepting our finitude is bringing greater appreciation to what's gone, and what still may be.

There's a beautiful story in Dr. Atul Gawande's book *Being Mortal* about a study in which people were asked with whom they wanted to spend time. They asked little kids, teenagers, adults, and then the elderly, and researchers found the trajectory went like this: little kids wanted to spend time with their family, teenagers wanted to spend time with their friends, and by the time you asked the guy in his thirties, he wanted to meet Bono. There are moments of our lives that fuel ambition and expansion and *more, more, more*. We can see a long future. But then the closer people grew to death, the more they wanted to spend time with their closest friends and family again. The horizon had expanded from childhood to adulthood, and then shrunk back to that beautiful, precious core.

What's delightful about this study of horizons is the way that age can teach us what to love. When we have more past than future, our desires may change to love

not simply what *might be,* but to love *what already is.*
Our nearest and dearest. The people we couldn't get rid
of if we tried. The ways our bodies and minds have carried us. The small moments of a single day.

Perhaps that is the best prayer of all. *God, give me
the desires of my heart,* only to discover that what you
desire is already there, holding your hand, complaining
about the weather because, hey, no one is perfect.

A Blessing for Loving What Is

Blessed are you who are attempting to love what is here, what is now. You who recognize the wonder and pain looking at life's rearview mirror, at those things that are gone. The person you were. The quickness and sharpness of a body that didn't tire as quickly. The relationships and jobs and aspirations. The people you can't get back. Blessed are you, holding the gentle compassion that wraps memories in grace.

And blessed are you, turning your gaze from imagined futures that seem to call out with an unnecessary pressure and an urgency that wants to rob you of what joys still exist. And oh how blessed are you, drawing a tidy boundary around today and calling it home. For yesterday is a memory, tomorrow a mirage.

Blessed are you, recognizing that the rightsizing of reach and possibility is the heart's ease of God's good counsel. Opening your eyes to all that is here. Let its beauty seep into your pores and whisper words of peace. Receive and welcome reality in its completeness, giving over to God all that is beyond your power to change or understand or return to once again. And in the meantime, embracing and loving the life you have, the family you have, the pleasures that are yours. Right now.

A GOOD ENOUGH STEP

Take a blank piece of paper and pen. Without thinking about what you will write, put your pen in motion and let it talk to you about what is here, right here and right now. Write letters and words and phrases; write the chaos that is your life. In all its strange detail. Use color words and emotion-laden adjectives and pile it all up, all the blessings that your pen knows about that you haven't thought of yet, or brought to mind for years. Draw a circle around it all. This is what is.

Then lift your pen, start in a new place, and let your pen make a word salad of desires. All of it. The things you have long hoped for, even the things that are now over. All your heart's deepest and most hidden longings. Let it flow. Then draw a circle around it all. This is what was, and what may be. They are here too, though hidden in memory or in desire.

And all of this—past, present, and future—is still you. It is the particularity that is your life. Precious beyond rubies. Utterly irreplaceable, indelible. Because as soon as you turn over the page and walk away, it is still there with you. So do it, turn the page, but keep the pen. It knows a lot.

"Yesterday is gone. Tomorrow has not yet come. We have only today. Let us begin."

—MOTHER TERESA, *In the Heart of the World: Thoughts, Stories, and Prayers*

23

BEING HONEST ABOUT DISAPPOINTMENT

Today might be the kind of day when you are feeling it most—the loneliness that comes with suffering. That's because it is yours alone. No one else can see with your eyes, or feel what you feel.

I remember a moment when I was about to be wheeled into surgery and, for some reason, I could suddenly remember every line of a poem by Ella Wheeler Wilcox I had memorized in the fifth grade. The poem loudly declares that in times of pleasure and plenty, we are surrounded by others. But when we must go through suffering, "we must all file on through the narrow aisles of pain."

I said the words very loudly and very formally, as poetry demands, and a nurse paused to look at me with great concern. BUT ISN'T THAT THE RIGHT THOUGHT? When the suffering comes, your loss or grief or illness or disappointment forces you down a solitary path.

And if you are like me, that's when prayer sometimes adds to the loneliness. Where is God when you pray and ask for help, but it doesn't come? Why doesn't God answer? How can I believe in a God who doesn't seem to see me or hear me?

Illness, grief, or any kind of suffering in this world feels like it doesn't belong in a world made by a good God. It is just wrong. And painful. And frankly, sometimes just infuriating. I find myself praying, *God, the world really seems like a terrible character reference for You. I know people say You are good, but I don't see much evidence today.*

Acute suffering cries out for an answer. We need the pain to stop. *Right now!* Our urgent call longs to be met by a strong, wise, and loving answer. We want healing and answers and strength to go on. But so often, we hear nothing at all.

Instead of rushing to defend God or dissect the great mystery of the problem of evil, I have found it to be wonderfully freeing to begin with the truth. As my best friend likes to remind me on awful days:

You feel hurt, because it's painful.
You feel sad, because it's tragic.
You feel angry, because it's unfair.

You are okay to feel what you feel. We need freedom to acknowledge the brutality of life without minimizing or pretending or justifying. We need not rush to defend God or delude ourselves. It is terrible. And it is happening.

When I asked Father James Martin, author and Jesuit priest, about how I might pray in awful seasons—after pain, after disappointment—he suggested that I might be on the right track already. Prayer, he said, begins with acts of unbridled honesty. *God, this isn't enough. God, I can barely make it through the hour.*

I would prefer a world run by formulas. I am good, and therefore I will thrive. I am loving, so no one can leave me. I am hardworking, so I can never be slowed and stopped by sickness and death and disability and despair. The life I want is predictable, controllable, and fundamentally fair. But instead, I see that reality is infused by war and violence, illness and hurricanes.

And if you're wondering, yes. People love to hear this perspective at parties.

Just kidding.

But all the good things that can come from prayer— trust, acceptance, connection, occasional miracles—are there waiting for us. But first comes radical honesty. The more genuine our prayers, the more freedom there is to acknowledge the reality of all a life with God can be.

In the meantime, tell God. All of it. Fiercely. Even the unanswered prayers. Don't leave out a single one. Even if you sit among broken things and your confidence seems to shrink with each day, know that you may feel lonely but you are not alone. You are united in love with all of suffering humanity, and with our God who came to suffer and die. A God of sorrows, and acquainted with grief. But one who also came that we might have life.

A Blessing for When You're Disappointed

Blessed are you, dear one, when you don't know if you can pray. Because even that very thought is the beginning of prayer, whether you know it or not.

Blessed are you when you are disappointed, when you have prayed and hoped and wished, and still your cry for help goes unanswered. Blessed are you in the grip of the radical honesty that says, God, what are You doing? Why don't You answer? What is so hard about making something good happen, when I have laid it all out before You in all its terrible reality? Blessed are you, when you have lifted it all up to God and now must sit among the broken things and pray a one-word prayer of need. Help. Save. Come.

Blessed are you still there before God amid the unanswered prayers. For you are not alone. No. There is One who has come to feel what you feel, to suffer what you have borne. And this Jesus comes right to the heart of your pain. That's the place He knows best. And desires to transform with the blazing light of healing love. That's the only thing that makes the difference. That can drag you and me from the place of unrest.

Blessed are you, sweet child. Daring to ask, God, help me trust You, even if You never tell me why. Then settling yourself into the reality that God's hands are the safest place to be. And you pray again, Into Your hands, O Lord, I commend my spirit. Hide me in the shadow of Your wings.

A GOOD ENOUGH STEP

When was the last time you let yourself be honest with God? Really, radically, honest. Not just in your disappointments, but in your hopes too. What do you hope for that you are afraid to say aloud out of fear of being disappointed? What about the unanswered prayers you've grown tired of asking for? Tell God everything. Nothing is off-limits. Let the words hang in the air, even unanswered, full of all the frustration and desperation, anger and sorrow. Settle in. Take a deep breath. Trust that God hears, that God hasn't left your side. God can handle it all.

24

KINDNESS BOOMERANGS

"Be kind, for everyone you meet is fighting a hard battle."

—IAN MACLAREN

My parents have a wonderful tradition I didn't learn about until I was an adult. Every year on their anniversary, they go out to dinner to celebrate. But it isn't just dinner they look forward to. They begin to scope the room, reading the body language of their fellow diners. Once they pick their target, they conspire with the waiter: "See that irritable couple over there, the ones not talking to each other at all? We want to pay for their meal, and be out of the restaurant before they ask for their bill. This is to be totally anonymous." Usually, the waiter joins them in their sly glances and big grins and promises to let them know what the couple's order will be. They inevitably ask, "Do you do this often?" My parents smile. "It's tradition."

There is something about this type of kindness that reverberates. Not only is it something my parents look forward to each year, the waiters get in on it, and, hopefully, the person on the receiving end bumps their toe on goodness for a change. It is a strange kind of magic. It feels good to be kind. Even when it's done in secret.

Even when no one says thank you. Even when it isn't asked for or expected.

This kind of ripple effect has attracted the attention of researchers around the world. Some experiments involved handing out roses or offering free hugs. It's not a perfect science, but there is something about unexpected kindness that warms both the giver and the recipient.

One experiment focused on a robot. How might people respond if given a random chance to go out of their way? In 2009, the Tweenbots project decided to find out by researching real-time responses in Washington Square Park in the middle of New York City (Jessica's absolute favorite place to people-watch).

Imagine you are walking in Washington Square Park, under the Roman arch, around the fountains, enjoying the street performers, and you see a small robot made of cardboard moving aimlessly. It is rather adorable with eyes and a big painted-on smile. The robot holds a sign with a destination and the words HELP ME FIND MY WAY.

Would you slow your pace to guide a lost robot? Most people did! They were gentle and helpful, guiding the little robot across the park. In another version, the Tweenbot was sitting and held a sign that said PLEASE CALL MY FAMILY AND TELL THEM WHERE I AM, AND THAT I'M OK. There was a phone number to call. And people did.

That most people were willing to help a robot who

could offer nothing in return told the researcher Kacie Kinzer a lot about the degree to which people were willing to be kind.

Kindness is a restorative act done for the good of another, handing over something valuable without the expectation of return. And yet, it does offer us something. There is this unexpected boomerang effect. The day gets better—not always easier, definitely not perfect, but a bit *sweeter*. We remember that no matter what is happening in our own lives, in our own orbits, we have the capacity to add a little goodness into the world. What a surprise: give, and it will be given to you (Luke 6:38).

A Blessing Before You Act
with Kindness

Blessed are you who have tasted how good it is to bless, who have paused in wonder at the strange math where it is in giving that we receive. As we give, we begin to see in ourselves a tiny resemblance to our God, the Giver of Life. Blessed are we, who in giving, are being drawn closer. We begin to see life in relation to where God shows us we belong. We live more and more out of that inheritance we received through Jesus Christ, who gave his body. A real body, that ours might not die.

Blessed are we, drawn to the warmth that is this deep belonging.

So now we are beginning to understand blessing itself. The overabundance of delight that flows from the heart of God into our own. The excess of bliss that descended pure as a mountain stream to create all that is, and sustain it by love alone. Blessed are we, carried along in that flow. To love and give and give again. And when we are spent, to be gathered up and restored so we can love again. Bless again. And be blessed. Because that's why we were made in the first place.

> "He has told you, O mortal, what is good; and
> what does the Lord require of you but to do
> justice, and to love kindness, and to walk humbly
> with your God?" (Micah 6:8)

It's your turn to do a mysterious act of kindness.

Pay it forward at the coffee bar and walk away before the next person finds out who did it. Take a walk by the riverbank or in a park and secretly gather up and dispose of any trash you find—wear rubber gloves of course! Put the dishes into the dishwasher the way they like it—this one is harder to do anonymously, but it could work. And if no one notices, you can be sure that God did.

"What had been expended in kind-hearted faith never perishes before the Lord."—POPE LEO THE GREAT, Sermon 78

25

GIVE UP ALREADY

It's fashionable, at the moment, to talk about giving up, paring down, and letting things go. Capitalism is the great monster of acquisition, so we have a nagging feeling that perhaps part of the solution may involve making do with less. There are bestsellers galore to explain how to reduce time spent staring at your phone, online shopping, or eating carbs. Marie Kondo decided that there is a magical power to tidying up and made it her mission to help people declutter and keep only what sparks joy. In an era of *more,* there is wisdom in learning the value of *less.*

Christianity has a long tradition of asking people to loosen their tight grip on comfort by practicing giving something up. It is the tradition of fasting, and, quite frankly, it freaks many of us out. Fasts can be intermittent, seasonal, or targeting specific foods or drinks. It may remind us of preparing for the terrible pregnancy glucose test or getting ready for a physical or prepping for that surgery. Or something we tried once because a cousin bought a juicing machine and assured us that her new liquid diet was "medical." (Never mind that the fine "doctor" got his title from an online degree mill.)

Whatever other benefits (or absurdities) are related to fasting, the Christian tradition has always insisted that fasting has a spiritual purpose. In fact, Jesus took it for granted that his disciples would fast, telling them *"When* you fast . . ."

Not *"If* you fast . . ."

Or *"Consider trying* a fast . . ."

Or *"Maybe, someday, you might wonder about* fasting *on a strictly intellectual level . . ."*

Right from the start, it was assumed that fasting would be a regular part of the Christian life. When we fast, we imitate Jesus, who spent forty days fasting in the desert before beginning his public ministry. He chose to pursue God by setting aside comfort.

So what is fasting? Fasting is simply giving up something for a time. It's not a diet. It's not a punishment. It's not really meant to have any concrete benefit except the experience itself. Theologian Dietrich Bonhoeffer described it perfectly: somehow, in our giving up, we experience discipline and freedom.

Sounds like a contradiction, doesn't it?

But there is a strange liberation in letting things go. We loosen our attachment to what weighs us down, and it frees us from behaviors and habits that we would rather not admit out loud. So when we fast, as Bonhoeffer says, we are made into disciples "more ready and cheerful to accomplish those things which God would have done."

Fasting and cheerfulness may also sound like a wild contradiction. (Seriously, you don't want to see me before my morning coffee.) But something quite lovely happens when we let go, when we live with less, when we give up something dear. Somehow, we make a little room for God to take up more space. And wherever God is, that's where we want to be.

A Blessing Before a Fast

Blessed are you, ready to open yourself to a new joy, a doorway that until now has been hidden. In this culture of acquisition and gain, blessed are you who desire fresh ears to hear what might be a bit too loud. Who take the next step to turn it down a notch and make more space for God. Who discipline yourself, with time, intention, and hope, anticipating God to show up in your discomfort. Trusting that when we need God, God promises to be there.

God, give me courage, give me strength, give me hunger for You. Let this set time of less be a chance for more of You. Let this fast be an entrance into the discernment I desire, the divine presence I'm longing for, and the hope to will what You will, oh God, to be who You've called me to be.

A GOOD ENOUGH STEP

Ask God to show you something that will become a symbol of spiritual resilience, which will in turn be the springboard to joy. Remember: a fast is giving up something—anything—to make more room for God. It might be a break from social media or Netflix, caffeine, unkind words, alcohol, or holding a grudge. If you are someone who has a complicated relationship with restricting food, skip that for now. Try something else instead. Remember, this isn't about punishing yourself or a thinly veiled version of a diet. Share your intention with a friend to reinforce your commitment, but do your fast in secret—just between you and God. Try it out for a week, and then reassess.

"Do you want to fast this Lent?" asked Pope Francis.

Fast from hurting words and say kind words.
Fast from sadness and be filled with gratitude.
Fast from anger and be filled with patience.
Fast from pessimism and be filled with hope.
Fast from worries and trust in God.
Fast from complaints and contemplate simplicity.
Fast from pressures and be prayerful.
Fast from bitterness and fill your heart with joy.
Fast from selfishness and be compassionate to others.
Fast from grudges and be reconciled.
Fast from words and be silent so you can listen.

26

SAY POTATO

On the invitation to Kate's parents' wedding was a drawing of the portly Winnie-the-Pooh and his tiny friend Piglet walking hand in hand.

"It isn't much fun for One, but Two
Can stick together," says Pooh, says he.
"That's how it is," says Pooh.

Well, that's a lovely sentiment. But it's hard. It's hard to make two out of one.

I (Jessica) lived in the same place for twenty-five years. While Denver, Colorado, is a major city by all normal-people standards, it always felt like a small town to me. I can't pick up an iced coffee or get my tires rotated without running into someone I know. These are the kinds of friends who remember things I have tried very hard to forget. Like the time our parents wanted to infect us with chicken pox and made us share bubble gum, or when we danced to Madonna's "Like a Prayer" in the elementary school's talent show, or the time my car slammed into a fire hydrant. (I claim complete innocence and blame the person who never taught me how four-wheel drive works.) I had long, storied relationships with that city, with those people. But when I was an adult, I moved away.

Making friends as an adult is hard. Making friends as an adult in a new city is even harder. Especially when you work from home and have no discernible hobbies. I could be anyone I wanted to be, but there was something I missed about being *known*. I was fresh out of a marriage that had broken my heart, and I didn't know how to move past small talk. Intimacy with strangers felt like a risk my fragile self couldn't handle. I longed for the comfort of people with whom I could be real—in my grief and heartbreak and hope.

I was reminded of the difficulty of making genuine connections when I read a fascinating article by the writer CJ Hauser, who joined the dating app Tinder in order to find a potential match. She quickly found herself caught in the endless monotony of small talk. *How are you? What do you do? This weekend looks like nice weather.* So few people, she said, felt real.

Well, that's because they weren't necessarily real. She discovered a horrifying little fact: people on dating apps may be falling victim to a form of fraud. There are programmed scripts called Tinder bots that may look and sound like a real person but are actually a little algorithm designed to be spectacular at small talk. In fact, these fake bots are so common (and so persuasive!) that people have found themselves falling in love with "someone" created by artificial intelligence.

What a strange modern reality: with so many loose connections among people, our relationships have been weakened to the point where even robots can seem like convincing stand-ins.

But here is the heartening news—artificial intelligence can't duplicate human interaction perfectly. It's too smooth, too instant, and too incapable of understanding complex forms of communication like irony or hyperbole. And, to top it off, Tinder bots are not nearly as random as people. Humans go down conversational rabbit trails that make no sense to an algorithm.

Alan Turing, the father of computer science, had something to say about this. He helped the Allies crack Nazi codes, which, some argue, saved millions of lives by leading to a swifter end to World War II. His life's work wondered: Can machines think? He developed the Turing test to determine how a computer or bot could approximate human behavior. The Turing test was simple: if the human couldn't tell if they were talking to a computer or a person, the computer passed.

When CJ Hauser started to question the authenticity of her online relationships, she began to use a cheeky version of the Turing test, hilariously dubbed "The Potato Test." When she worried someone was overly automated, she would say, "If you're human, say 'potato.'"

Bots don't have a programmed response for something so absurd.

What exactly constitutes this uniquely human "thing" that can't be duplicated by artificial intelligence? Could it be the flaws? Our jokes that don't always land or our weird hobbies we wonder if anyone else will find entertaining? Is it in our silly stories or complicated families?

None of us is perfect, and somewhere in those imperfections we can be found.

Maybe it's true that it hurts a little to become real and risk intimacy with a stranger who might become that friend we're looking for. Or we might be the one they need at that precise moment. Perhaps it is our job to help one another become more real, one absurd question at a time.

So, my dears, if you need the reminder that love is found not in spite of our flaws but because of them, say, "Potato."

A Blessing for When You Feel Lonely

Oh God, blessed are we who call to You for help when life's solitary candle burns too low. You know our frame, You remember we are dust. Tell me it was not for nothing that we were made.

Blessed are we who cry out: God, I need a friend to share the simple unaffected joys that come, the troubles unbidden, those too heavy to sustain.

I lift my face to You and ask that with those pierced hands You would hold me, and trace each tear to its source. Oh God, heal me, restore me, and provide for me, so even the memory of this loneliness is forgotten.

Awaken me to life. To warmth and faith and hope and love that shines unknowingly on the path of others, and smiles to find it shining freely back.

Blessed are we, opening our hands in readiness to risk intimacy, to receive the gift of friendship and give it in return. *Amen.*

A GOOD ENOUGH STEP

Write a terrible poem about longing for a friend. Write freely, not worrying about having to share it with anyone else. I recommend writing it down on a physical piece of paper. You'll be less tempted to edit yourself and you'll lean into that stream of consciousness. I try to write and edit in two entirely different settings as each one uses a different part of my creative brain. Try that now.

Before you delete it or throw it away or forget about it, notice what it says about your needs and desires. Do you want a friend to walk with, or one who wouldn't mind a surprise phone call, or another who likes the same music or author? Do you need encouragement, a birthday party, help moving? Write a specific prayer that asks for a friend for each type of interest, need, or desire. What comes to mind? Is there someone you could reach out to who might just fit one of these interests? Is there someone who has reached out to you lately to whom you might reciprocate? Take a risk. Be ready to move on to the next if that one isn't what you'd hoped for.

"Vulnerability is for the brave." —LIDIA LONGORIO, *Hey Humanity*

27

TO MY BODY

Dear Body,

Sometimes, I hate you. You ache. You get tired sooner than I'd like to admit. You wake me in the night for no good reason. Your cells duplicate at unpredictable rates. New gray hairs and fine lines and silver stretch marks show up out of nowhere. You let me down just when I need you the most.

Sometimes, I look in the mirror and don't recognize the person staring back at me. I look exhausted. Worn. Aged.

Sometimes, I want a break from living with you. I'd prefer to trade you in for a newer model. A model that isn't in constant pain, that fits better in that pair of jeans, that has more energy. With you, I am limited— bound by skin and bone and thinning hair.

With you, I am fragile.

It wasn't always this way. I remember when you had invisible springs. You didn't need coaxing, tending, or fixing. You had endless courage and resilience. You could stay up all night with a friend or chase littles around in the yard. You seemed invincible, your memory, infallible.

Yet here we are. This flesh and bone. These cages.

These places of freedom and constraint. I want my body to be perfect, but instead I'm reminded of what I can't master, what I cannot perfect.

But God knows what it's like to live in flesh. God went to great, even incarnational, lengths to be born as a tiny infant (John 1:14). If God too lived in a body, then God knows the ache of growing pains and the feeling of goosebumps on a brisk day and the comfort of a warm embrace. He felt the gurgle of a hungry stomach and the annoying prick of a splinter after a day of hard work. He wept over the death of a friend. Ours is a God who sneezed and rubbed His eyes when He was sleepy. Ours is a God who knew longing, heartbreak, excitement, frustration—the full range of what it means to be human. A God who knows what it means to live in a body.

So when my own body drags me down, when my muscles ache, when my worries keep me up at night, when my fear for the future leaves me motionless, when I feel lonely and exhausted and burdened, I do not worship a God who is far off.

This is a God who knows my humanity inside and out. God has counted every hair on my head (Matthew 10:30) and bottled up every tear I have shed (Psalm 56:8). Not simply because the Word formed us (Genesis 1:27), knit us together in our mothers' wombs (Psalm 139:13), was there from the very beginning . . . but because God wore our skin.

Dear, dear body, I get it. Or at least I am starting to. You do not have an unlimited supply. You run out, and I need to listen. Maybe I really should go to bed a little earlier or let you off the hook for craving those extra salty chips. I need to sense when you are struggling, and gently acknowledge that you are actually changing. That time and love and grief and life have worn themselves into my skin. Day by day. This is the beautiful, terrible evidence that we have lived.

So, let's give up the myth of perfection, shall we? Perfection in what we eat. Perfection in what we assume bodies should look like or feel like. Perfection in imagining we'd be over this weird body stuff by now.

So, I want to say I am sorry. You couldn't help aging, changing, being human. I love you. I will try to be gentle and patient with your ways.

So, dear body, let us quiet ourselves and look to God who made us in all our imperfections and in our total dependence. Through God, in God, we live and move and find our being (Acts 17:28). Let us be more awake, more alive, more drawn together body and soul into that single purpose—to love and be loved by a God who calls us God's own.

And let us remember that this fragile body is good enough.

Love always,
Me

A Blessing for the Body

Blessed is the body that offers soft hugs on hard days. Whose curves fit our pets and our kids and our partners. Whose hands hold another alongside hospital beds and in nursing homes and at the altar and on the first day of school. Whose breasts nurse and legs run to chase littles and whose toes balance us on the earth. Whose wrinkles tell stories of laughs and tears and worries.

Blessed are these imperfect, fragile bodies. This flesh and bone. These cells that sometimes duplicate for no reason whatsoever. This skin that is stitched together with scars and stretch marks and fine lines.

Blessed is the body because it is a home. Not just for us, but for those who love us. And sometimes you just need to stand in front of the mirror and take off all your clothes, and remember that this body, your body, is God's home address.

A GOOD ENOUGH STEP

Love can be infused from both the outside in as well as from the inside out. Rub lotion on your arms and legs. Massage your feet. Give yourself a hug. Marinate in God's love for your skin and bone. The God who came in flesh loves you—just as you are—and made you in God's image. Read Psalm 139 as you reflect on what it means that God loves even your body.

"Enjoy your body. Use it every way you can. Don't be afraid of it or of what other people think of it. It's the greatest instrument you'll ever own."

—MARY SCHMICH, "Wear Sunscreen"

28

MEDIOCRITY FOR THE WIN

Sometimes we are convinced that we're not good enough.

Take my great-grandmother Marjorie Bebbington, for instance. She was born in England around 1904. No one is sure exactly because she was daughter *number four* and there was such a fuss about what to do with her because her dad had plain run out of names for girls. Apparently, you can run out. Of names, and of energy to pay attention to "another fiddlin' female," or so her father called her. Marjorie grew up knowing that she was both too much and not enough.

But my great-grandmother Gi-Gi, as we called her, was a hell of a woman. She was tough and kind and didn't let anything stop her.

She was the custodian of an entire apartment block, took care of her entire family, sewed and knitted every piece of their clothing, and still made their lunch every day to order. Bacon on the side, that kind of thing.

She loved to smoke, even though she thought none of us knew, and when she finally got around to something she *couldn't* do—which is to say she was a *deeply* mediocre painter—she had a solution for that too. She went to the secondhand store and bought an oil painting. Then she found a matching color and painted her name right over the artist's signature in the bottom right-hand corner.

Ta-da!

I had that one hung in my house until I got old enough to think . . . wait a minute . . . she really made some remarkable progress.

My great-grandmother had bought into a story of intense perfectionism: that she had to be everything, or she was nothing at all.

We are living in a culture that celebrates the high-stakes qualities of perfectionism. Researchers have been following the rise of unrealistic and self-critical standards as a kind of societal phenomenon. Job applicants trying to impress the new boss cite "trying too hard" as the only acceptable humblebrag. Mental health experts describe anxiety and low self-esteem as the result of ever-increasing standards of physical, social, and emotional perfectionism. We are living in an unending pageant and the judges never tire.

Even churches have adopted the language of our striver society. When I was researching megachurches, one of the primary slogans from the pulpit was that their church was defined by their "culture of excellence." Who can forget Winners Church and their slogan "Where winning is a lifestyle!"?

We are nothing if we are not perfect.

But then we fail. Or we are frozen in our fear of being imperfect. We have googled "impostor syndrome" too many times and wonder if our successes are deserved or our inevitable descent is just around the corner.

If only we could trust that the giving of ourselves, with all our imperfections, has a value beyond rubies. We need a deep permission. Permission to ask for help. Permission to get better. Permission to fail.

If Marjorie Bebbington were still alive, I would take a tour through her life to tell her what was perfect—not for the delicate oil painting in all its fraudulent glory. I would remind her that she was a wonderful cook and a better person, had a soft heart and a quick mind. And, pointing to another of her paintings—a crudely rendered bunch of yellow daisies—I would tell her that the best part about her wasn't the best at all. It wasn't even great. But the best part about her was that the way she tried and lived and loved was her true art.

A Prayer for When You Feel Like You're Not Enough

Dear God,

What is this strange unease? It feels like restlessness, but it's more than that. It's the sense that some unnamed standard is convincing me that I will never be enough. Smart enough. Pretty enough. Healthy enough. Young enough. Brave enough. Grateful enough. I have come to the end of myself. I am not enough.

There are cracks in everything, but You fill them with love. Fill me with Your divine presence that is entirely unimpressed by my attempts at perfection. God, sing over me the truth of how You see me. You made me in love, for love, and—somehow—it is enough.

Blessed are we who see that intrinsic worth comes, not through our talents, but from You. Thank You for saving me from my own dreams of perfection.

Amen.

A GOOD ENOUGH STEP

You are made to hear God. And strangely, God speaks through things we can see. Psalm 19 says, "The heavens are telling the glory of God; the skies proclaim the work of his hands. Day after day they pour forth speech." God is on display everywhere we cast our eyes.

Contemplating art can be a spiritual practice, an act of divine seeing. It's called Visio Divina. Let's try it. Pick an image. It can be art you have on your wall, or you can pull up something online, or head to a local art exhibit, or visit an outdoor mural. Settle in. Ask God to reveal God's self through the work of art. Rest your eyes on the image and drink it in for several minutes. How do you feel? If you are in this image, where are you? Are there words that arise from this practice? What is God showing you?

Take, for example, Caravaggio's painting *The Incredulity of Saint Thomas,* where Jesus guides the hand of his trembling disciple into his wounded side. The pale skin reminds us that Jesus has newly come from the valley of the shadow of death, to overcome not only death but the fear of it, the finality of its devastating impact. Or look at the illuminations of *The Saint John's Bible,* where in lettering of gold and pigments of bold hue, the word of God takes on visual shape that gleams from the calfskin pages. This is the work of looking in order to hear. To hear what God will say. Look long. It is there, the perfection that we can never achieve, but that has been lavishly given.

"What a rich wisdom it would be, and how much more bountiful a harvest, to gain pleasure not from achieving personal perfection but from understanding the inevitability of imperfection and pardoning those who also fall short of it."

—BARBARA KINGSOLVER, *Small Wonder*

29

THE BURDEN OF LOVE

Why is it that grief feels so much like fear?

That is a question that you don't expect an author like C. S. Lewis to be asking, especially if you have read his many children's books, where good always wins. In his Narnia tales like *The Lion, the Witch and the Wardrobe,* the evil white witch is overpowered by the untamable Aslan.

But in *A Grief Observed,* Lewis allows himself to ask the questions poured from the deepest parts of his pain. Two things had suddenly collided in his life: Just as he realized he was in love with his friend Joy, he was about to lose her.

Their deep intellectual friendship became almost incandescent with love. As Joy's son later described, "They seemed to walk together within a glow of their own making." But as they were declaring their love and exchanging their vows, Joy was diagnosed with terminal cancer. They would have only three years of happiness and sorrow together.

Grief and love had created the space they had inhabited together, a space that Lewis now had to occupy alone. He writes, "I am not afraid, but the sensation is like being afraid. The same fluttering in the stomach, the same restlessness . . ." He describes his ache as a kind of suspense—so many habits, so many outcomes—stopped in midair. A world he had loved was impossible now, because of what has changed.

Lewis tried to draw a map of what was happening—first to understand it himself, and then, perhaps, to help others experiencing the same bewildering new reality of love lost.

But what Lewis discovered was not a map, not even a state of being, but a process. Grief couldn't be charted because it couldn't be pinned down. It didn't need a map, but rather a history. There was something new to be described every day. But not controlled. Oh no. Grief has a mind of its own. Lewis explained how loss leads you down deep ravines that descend in winding circles. It brings you to eerily normal spaces where it seems you can breathe again, like you always did, but then suddenly you're crying like you're eight years old. Then, without any warning, it takes your hand and settles you silently into something like joy made holy—wordless, indefinable, more real than your memories somehow.

"There is nothing we can do with suffering, except to suffer it," says Lewis.

When we have lost someone, advice from other people can sound a lot like white noise. *She's in a better place. At least he is not suffering anymore.* A veil seems to descend between the grief-stricken and everybody else in the normal world. It makes us yearn for communities who carve out space for mourning, like the Jewish custom of "sitting shiva," where friends and family gather for seven days together. Or how people in Greece and Portugal encourage widows to wear black for months, creating a reminder for others of their loss.

We all need a bit of permission to allow ourselves time and space to feel the weight of loss, and move through it in our own way. So my dears, what can then be said of grief except that it is the burden of love? It can't be defined or drawn, only suffered. But what must be said, what must be given, is the permission to feel it. All of it. Not as a state, but as a process. No one can tell you what that process must be for you, just now. So gently, gently, let it lead you through.

A Blessing for When You're in Grief

Blessed are you, dear one, in that place you don't recognize, where the landscape feels hostile and you are fumbling around in the darkness. Everything feels wrong. Because something important has died. Or someone is now gone. That one who filled the space that was beautiful and meaningful. How can the world continue to spin when mine has stopped?

Blessed are you, dear heart, grieving that which feels irreplaceable. And you are right to think so. Don't let anyone place upon you any other truth, but know this utterly.

Blessed are you under the burden of all that love. Because bearing it along with you is the faithful path for you to walk now. And even if you take a break and cook breakfast or buy flowers or laugh at a silly joke, it isn't breaking faith. It's the rest that pays tribute in its own way. It's the replenishing that is needed in order to continue, to press on and through and meet all the landmarks that tell you things are not the same. And you remember all over again, and it is still wrong.

Blessed are you, dear, dear one, doing this holy work of suffering what must be suffered. Of grieving what has been lost. Of knowing the unthinkable truth that must be known. This grief can make you feel on the other side of glass from the world around you, a force field separating your different realities. Yet blessed are you in your reality, for yours is the one most seen by God, who breathes compassion upon you, even now. Who has walked this path, and who leans toward you, gathering you up into the arms of love. Rest now, dear one. You are not alone. *Amen*.

A GOOD ENOUGH STEP

Go on a prayer walk. Let the prayers be spontaneous. Sit down and rest if you find a bench along the way. Hear the birds or cicadas or frogs. Listen as their songs become prayers. Add yours to the chorus.

"Where you used to be,
there is a hole in the world,
which I find myself constantly walking around in the daytime,
and falling in at night.
I miss you like hell."

—EDNA ST. VINCENT MILLAY, *Letters of Edna St. Vincent Millay*

30

REFUGE

There are stories we tell each other all the time. Not *lies* exactly, but stories. Truths we can live with.

I'm fine!
It's probably for the best.
It's all going to work out.

Before we know it, a partial truth has become a lie. You're not telling your friends that you're overwhelmed. You've stopped describing pain or addiction or a broken heart. You don't feel nearly as entitled to the full spectrum of emotions—from joy to sorrow—that you wouldn't mind hearing from a loved one. In an effort to save yourself (and others) from pain, sometimes you start to hit the mute button on your own life.

The psalms are these poems and prayers that express raw emotion. They cry out in anger. They rage against their enemies. They ask God for help. They weep and mourn. They blame God for not showing up soon enough.

The psalms remind us that God can take it *all*.

All our anger. All our shock. All our confusion. All our sorrow. All our shame. All our fear. All our grief. There is no need to tie a bow around what we feel or make ourselves more presentable to God. Nothing is off-limits. We can let it all pour out.

In Psalm 46, we read a song of holy confidence that expresses the ways that, even as the world falls apart in front of our very eyes, God's presence remains. They sing,

> *"God is our refuge and strength,*
> *an ever-present help in trouble.*
> *Therefore we will not fear, though the earth give*
>   *way*
> *and the mountains fall into the heart of the sea,*
> *though its waters roar and foam*
> *and the mountains quake with their surging."*
>   *(Psalm 46:1–3)*

The psalmist acknowledges the realities that surround us. He does not say, "When everything goes exactly as we planned, then you know God is with you." Or "Your life will always be evidence of God." Or "When things aren't going your way, blame yourself. After all, God is always working out everything for the good of those who love God."

No. It says the mountains are swallowed up by the depths. The earth crumbles under your toes. Though nations are at war. And kingdoms and cities go bankrupt. Though the world as we know it has been upended, it is *right there* we can find shelter with God, our refuge. God is our safe place, not after the worst is over or before the other shoe drops. But right *in the midst of* our pain and grief and loss.

God is our place of peace as the world around us rages on.

There is an eschatological tone here, a future-leaning vision that the psalmist is invoking. We are peering into a divine reality we can't quite see. The earth crumbles and somehow God is in our midst. Troubles tear down our lives and yet God is sheltering us with strength and safety and love.

When despair has stolen your hope or grief has ripped your heart from your chest or you desperately miss someone you can't get back, God is there. When you feel alone or terrified of your own mind, God is there. When you're drowning in an addiction you can't shake or you are undone by worry, God is still there.

Right in the midst of the trouble, God is with you. You are never alone.

A Prayer for After a Loss

God of all mystery, whose ways are greater than our ways, we don't know why things didn't get better. Why addiction wouldn't let him go. Why we couldn't save her. Why the disease took hold. Why the medicine didn't work. Why the accident happened to us.

They were too young. It was too soon. We
    weren't ready.
We need Your presence.
Be with us.
When the nights grow dark and our fears loom
    large,
Be with us.
When we face anniversaries and birthdays and
    holidays without the person we love,
Be with us.
When we make new memories, wishing they
    were here,
Be with us.

In the midst of the overwhelming love turned
    into grief,
May we find stillness in Your presence, oh God,
Our mighty fortress,

Our strong refuge,
Our enduring peace.

Be with us.

Oh God of refuge
lead us in hope,
this day and all our days.
We cannot do this without You.

Amen.

A GOOD ENOUGH STEP

When you don't know the words to pray, when your mind stirs and spins, when darkness threatens to shadow over you, will you cling to God as your refuge, as your place of peace as the world rages on?

There is a grounding prayer practice based on Psalm 46:10 that is easy to remember.

Close your eyes. Take some deep breaths. As you do, say these words . . . slowing your breath down, breathing deeper and deeper with every repetition, dropping a word with every exhale.

Be still and know that I am God
Be still and know that I am
Be still and know
Be still
Be

An urban myth says that William Shakespeare left his mark on Psalm 46. He was, it was said, forty-six years old at the time the translation was being commissioned by King James I. The forty-sixth word from the top is *shake* and the forty-sixth word from the bottom is *spear*. Coincidence? I thinketh not. But Kate's historian father says this is bosh and flimshaw and must be expunged posthaste.

31

BOTTLING MAGIC

Sometimes I wish there was a cell phone app that would let you know the moment of peak delight in a day. That moment when you took the perfect bite of a gorgeous meal. Or when a friend's joke made you laugh until you couldn't catch your breath. Or your kid gave you a hard hug out of nowhere. Or you had a revelation at work that clicked everything into place. Wouldn't it be nice to have a little *ping* when the day crescendos? Something to remind you to notice, drink it in, be grateful. *Beep!* It's happening right now. This is it. *Pay attention.*

When something is that good, the temptation is to keep it, hold it, bottle it, preserve it, and, if we're the entrepreneurial type, maybe even sell it. But often, those precious moments are fleeting. They are precious exactly *because* they are few and far between.

A less-than-outdoorsy person went on a walk (okay, it was me, Jessica. I hate being outside, a strange sentiment, I know, especially for someone from Colorado where Subarus are a state residency requirement). But this day felt different. I had been cooped up, like so many others, for weeks. The weather had been gloomy for days that strung together, one after another. The cloudiness reflected inside too. But, then, finally, the sun broke. So I took a walk. There was a slight breeze. The cherry blossoms, Japanese magnolias, dogwoods, and redbuds were in full bloom. The smell of wisteria filled the air. I felt filled to the brim by the sun and blooms. It felt like *magic*.

But then, you try to go back, and the weather won't cooperate. The birds may not sing. You get sunburnt. Or your sneakers give you blisters. Once-gorgeous flowers are blown nude. You might be particularly grumpy that day. Or a friend may cancel, leaving you to wander alone.

That's the tension. Being outside doesn't *guarantee* magic. And neither does parenting or cooking or spending time with friends or painting or praying. This is the problem with these small glimpses. We want to instrumentalize the moment. We want to stay there. When something is good, we want to build a fortress—move in and live there forever.

Jesus's disciples knew something about this impulse. There is this odd story in the Gospels about when Jesus takes a few of his best friends on a hike up a mountain. There they see something quite remarkable, something they too were tempted to bottle up. Jesus's clothing becomes dazzling white. His face changes. Moses and Elijah appear from beyond the grave. The dazed disciples realize they are in the presence of the divine. Heaven touches earth in one transcendent moment. The rather impulsive of the bunch, Peter, offers to build three tabernacles right then and there. Three dwelling places to house Jesus and his ghostly friends. His reaction is one we may recognize. *Can we make this moment last longer?*

God has the habit of breaking into our lives in the most unpredictable of ways. Sometimes it's on mountaintops or through the super-spiritual act, like a sermon or prayer. Other times it comes after reading a line from a poem, or during a conversation with an old friend that makes you feel known. Maybe it is while you are on a run, or trying to paint, or over the dinner table with your grandkids. The transcendence is random and fleeting. Here now, gone tomorrow.

As hard as we try, we can't put it in a tower and build a fortress around it. And even if we could, the spark would have moved on. Everyday magic would lose its wonder.

We can't bottle the magic. But we can learn to see the signs, to feel the moments swell around us. We begin to see those brief periods as delicate, precious: here today and gone tomorrow. We can become more beautiful, more transcendent, as we learn to carry them with us, changed by the things we might never see again.

A Blessing for a Magic Moment

Blessed are we who recognize that spark, that glimmer of transcendence that feels . . . otherworldly. Like points of light that converge to reveal a reality we can scarcely believe, yet somehow we remember in the depths of our souls. The sunrise that no picture can capture. The moment of clarity we can't exactly describe. The quality time with a friend that we can't duplicate. It is a magic suffused with delight and goodness and beauty and joy. And we know it was You, oh God.

Blessed are we, more alive to the desire that has been awakened. And our desire becomes longing, and longing, faith in the certainty of things unseen.

Blessed are we who stand here, on this bedrock, glad to gaze toward what light remains even now, with grateful hearts.

Amen.

A GOOD ENOUGH STEP

Some seasons, the moments of God's presence are evident . . . and other times God seems far off. The ancient Israelites needed reminders of God's presence for when they had forgotten. So, the prophet Samuel took a stone and marked the memory of God's help for all of Israel to remember. He called it an Ebenezer. (You can read about this in 1 Samuel 7:12.)

As an act of remembering, make your own Ebenezer. Find a stone outside. Think of a moment you last sensed the transcendence of God. Using a permanent marker, write one word on the rock that helps you remember this moment of magic. Place the stone somewhere (inside or out) that will help you remember every time you see it.

No, we can't bottle these moments, but we can be changed by them.

"Never forget:
we walk on hell,
gazing at flowers."

—KOBAYASHI ISSA, in *The Dumpling Field*

32

GONDOLA PRAYERS

When I was five years old our family went on one of those gondolas up a mountain in British Columbia, Canada, and at the very moment our cable car was suspended over the deepest part of the valley below, it stopped. It swayed at first, and then all went still. Nobody spoke. Except for a little voice (and yes it was mine): "How do we know this is on tight?"

That's the question, isn't it, when life gets real? When you are dangled over the abyss and there's nothing between you and . . . the thing everyone is thinking. We wonder, will this work the way it should? Are we okay?

Of course, that's when we really start praying it *is* on tight. *For everyone's sake.* In the face of such uncertainty, sometimes all we can do is pray.

But what are we actually doing when we pray? And what did the writer of the New Testament book of James mean when he told his fellow Christians that "the prayer of the righteous is powerful and effective"?

Experience tells us that prayer isn't a secret remote control we can use to zap reality to our liking. Sometimes we pray and nothing changes. Sometimes prayers lead to miracles. But there is a theodicy issue (about the persistence of evil in the world) at stake in the question of prayer. As I look back on my five-year-old self hanging over a deep ravine, it would be a perverse God indeed who said: "Be good enough and pray in the right way for it to be okay."

God, are You listening? Was I supposed to do something special to get Your attention?

What I love about history is that it anchors us in a reality we couldn't otherwise touch. The book of James offers practical advice to newly converted Christians about a foreign concept of worship. In their world, people prayed to chosen or local gods or goddesses: women swore by Artemis or Diana, Hercules was especially venerated in Thebes, and Ares in Sparta. The biblical author reminds them that they are not praying to fitful and bad-tempered gods who will punish them if they are angered. We are under the eye of the one true God who revealed salvation to us as a little baby, who knows us and loves us and hears our prayers.

This fact changed everything about prayer, for first-century Christians, and for us. Because since all things exist in relation to this God of love, our prayers do too.

We are praying to the God whose very sweetness has broken through to us.

So when *this* God moves to put our prayers into effect, they work powerfully. But we don't make them so. So what are we doing when we pray?

Somehow, we are touching a reality beyond the senses.

Did you know that it isn't your eyes that see? It's the

brain. I read a fascinating article in *The New Yorker* by Nicola Twilley called "Seeing with Your Tongue." A person experiencing blindness could learn to see with a device called a BrainPort. The sense of touch takes the place of the optic nerve, transporting images to the brain. And somehow, perception is translated.

I can't help but think that prayer works something like this. In prayer, we are brought into the presence of God, whose eternal reality translates for us. We sense that we were created because we are loved. Just that. We are not a means, but an end. And we are more whole, more alive, with a wellness that we didn't create through some transactional effort on our part.

And there is some waiting necessary. To pray means we have to yield up space and time, and some of our darling preoccupations. For one hot minute there is a self-emptying that mirrors God's own.

The mystery of prayer is that we may never understand exactly how it works, just that it draws us into intimacy with a God who hears. When even in our tiniest voices we wonder, "How do we know that this is on tight?" and we can expect, somehow, that someone hears us and answers: "I know, right?"

A Prayer for When You Don't Know How to Pray

_____

God, I don't know how to pray. Here I am, in the dark, without words. Praying with need so deep I can hardly see it or say it. Praying though prayer feels hopeless.

God, could You pray for me? Could You come into this space I am holding and speak the words so they echo through me and back to Your heart? Will Your Spirit intercede on my behalf, interpreting the groans I can't put into syllables and sounds?

God, I feel hidden away so deeply that I can't see very far, but I ask You, God, can You come find me here?

I am reaching out a hand, eyes closed, trusting for the moment when the next step seems possible, seems safe. And until then, I long to just feel You near.

Amen.

A GOOD ENOUGH STEP

Practice Lectio Divina, an ancient spiritual practice that understands scripture as a way to meet God. It begins with prayer, asking that God speak to you through the words of the text. This is followed by a slow reading of scripture. The words are meditated on, prayed over, held up to the light, contemplated. Read Psalm 5:1–7 as if you've never heard it before. Read it again and see if one phrase jumps out at you and seems to demand attention. Read it again and check to see if memories or thoughts arise as a result, and ask God what it means for your life. Listen, and respond, having a conversation with God. Read it again and be with God, and rest.

"Grace fills empty spaces, but it can only enter where there is a void to receive it, and it is grace itself which makes this void." —SIMONE WEIL, *Love in the Void: Where God Finds Us*

33

THE COST OF CARING

When I was young and joyfully selfish, my parents were very insistent that I learn to be charitable. The Christian tradition asks that you give ten percent of your earnings away to something that is decidedly *not* about your happiness, and so I was stuck taking a dime from every dollar earned doing chores to put in a separate piggy bank. At some point I had at least twenty dollars in coins, which I gave to the Salvation Army with a great deal of personal fanfare. *You're welcome. Yes, I'm always this magnanimous.*

We were even forced to do this family tradition where we had to shop for the Christmas wish list of another family. My parents, who had very little money to spare, would foot the bill. As I was piling presents into the shopping cart, marveling at my own generosity at their expense, I paused to ask my father, "How will we know when it's enough?"

"Give until it hurts," he said. "Then give a little bit more."

In the last decade or so, our culture has become increasingly ambivalent about whether our values should hurt or not. Shouldn't everything make us happy? Doesn't this violate the inviolable Laws of Self-Care? Our culture is so obsessed with boundaries that it pretends we can be untouched by pain and have lives of profound meaning. Take a bath! Call a friend! Wait, didn't you want to help save the environment too?

Part of the confusion here lies in our understanding of the purpose of pain. Much pain can and should be avoided, even prevented. Abusive relationships. Self-harm. Brokenness and dysfunction and pathologies of all kinds. That kind of pain is not part of God's desire for us and violates the deepest, truest thing about us: that we are deeply worthy of all good things. Full stop.

But there are some virtues we can develop, a people we can become, that require sacrifice. They are not easy flowers. They are like ridiculous hydrangeas, unnecessarily beautiful and temperamental as heck. When we want to grow, there might need to be some pruning. Some hacking at deadening habits and beliefs. Some watering and readjusting so we might grow toward the light.

I didn't understand until I met nurses that the good work was always going to be costly.

My friend Christie Watson is a writer and nurse in the United Kingdom. She had taken a step away from the hospital in order to teach nursing for several years, but during the pandemic she volunteered to serve on the front lines once again. She absolutely didn't have to, but she felt the overwhelming desire to be of service. The days and nights were grueling, and the death toll was staggering. Christie was exhausted but undeterred. She explained the brutality this way: the way you know you are doing your job correctly is that it costs you a part of your own soul. Even with the best self-care practices, the job of any caring professional—be it a nurse or doctor or social worker or teacher or chaplain—comes at a steep price. It costs you to care. Caring, she said, is an occupational hazard.

What will good things cost us?

Hope costs us the satisfaction of cynicism.

Love costs us selfishness.

Charity costs us greed. Which is *fun,* let us be clear. Didn't you see the 1980s Wall Street movies? You could be renting a money hurricane at this very moment!

We often see this cost clearly when we feel the weight of our obligations, whether it is in our careers or in our own homes—caring for our kids or aging parents or a disabled spouse. There is no amount of bubble bath—no matter how delicious the scent—that will generate the kind of empathy this work requires. The beautiful, terrible work of seeing one another's humanity up close.

A Blessing for When Caring Costs You

Blessed are you who want your life to count, you who do the right things, who hope it will all add up to something. That is some good math.

But blessed are you who do terrible, terrible math. You who care about strangers. What a waste—that wasn't going to get you a nicer apartment. You who give your health in service of people who might not even deserve it and who never say thank you. You could have been protecting yourself or, God forbid, sleeping through the night. But you are here instead.

Blessed are you who listen to long, winding stories from lonely hearts instead of rushing off to more interesting friends. You picked boredom or loving strangers instead of the warmth of being known. That was your time and you're never going to get it back.

Blessed are you who love people who aren't grateful, the sick who endanger your health, the deeply boring who know you have things to do. Loving people can be the most meaningful thing in the world, but it can also be hard and scary and boring and disgusting or sad or anxiety-inducing with zero overtime.

So bless you, dear one. You who made these bad investments, those acts of love that are not going to add up to success in the way the world sees it. You are the definition of love.

A GOOD ENOUGH STEP

Welcome to the Ministry of Encouragement! It's very straight-forward: think of someone who is having a difficult time. Maybe it's personal or work-related. Maybe they have a chronic ill-ness or are facing a long-haul kind of disease. Maybe they are in a care-oriented job and may need a little reminder that they are loved. Send a meal. Offer to mow the lawn or clean their house. Give them a gift card for groceries. Babysit, if it isn't too weird. Pop a note in the mail. Have flowers waiting for them on their porch. Send them an encouraging text or email with the phrase "No need to reply" inside. Give the gift of en-couragement. You'll love it or hate it, but you'll be good at it.

"But if anyone has the world's goods and sees his brother in need, yet closes his heart against him, how does God's love abide in him? Little children, let us not love in word or talk but in deed and in truth." (1 John 3:17–18)

There's a choice implied in this advice from the old man, John the Apostle. He lived so long that when he could no lon-ger walk, he was carried into the church to preach. Near the end of his life, his sermons were short and repetitive: "Little children, love one another." He would say it over and over until his disciples questioned him about it.

"If you do this, it is enough."

It's enough because it is all. It is the choice that prefers another to . . . any other thing you'd rather be doing at that moment. And it may be costly. When doing the loving thing becomes your way of moving in the world, suddenly there will be someone who comes into view whose need you can fill, whose life you can bless in simple but telling ways. When you love your neighbor, you are loving God, for it is the face of Jesus in the one who is sick, the stranger, the lonely, or the imprisoned. And strangely, it is in the act of giving that you receive joy.

Somehow, we are more blessed when we give than when we receive. So, all things considered, even if this were a cost-benefit analysis, giving is a price worth paying.

THE REALITY-SHOW GOSPEL

My friends and I play this game whenever we watch reality television. We send each other clips of the stars claiming "Everything Happens for a Reason."

This is The Reality-Show Gospel. No seriously. Listen for it. You will be amazed at how pervasive this cultural myth is.

It tends to come up when someone has been dumped or when a contestant was voted out before their time or when a lover was jilted at the altar but now has the amazing new opportunity to find their soulmate on some far-off island. (All the while, they have become Instagram royalty, but of course they are in it "for the right reasons.") They've gained "perspective" and realize that everything must turn out okay, so therefore, this negative thing that happened must bring about something better.

And this script seems to work perfectly . . . until it doesn't. Until you receive a diagnosis or a divorce blows up your family or you hear that he or she is gone. Until your baby is born without a heartbeat. Until a friend is killed in a senseless accident. Until you lose your job unexpectedly. Until. Until. Until.

What about when there are no reasons to be found? And the hunt for explanation does more harm than good?

A well-meaning neighbor stopped by the house in the wake of my diagnosis to drop off a casserole. She reassured my husband, "Well, everything happens for a reason!"

"Oh really? I'd love to hear it. I'd love to hear the reason my wife is dying," he answered dryly, staring her dead in the eye.

The neighbor stumbled over a response and backpedaled into the safety of her own home. *Who knew that peace-loving Mennonites could bring the heat?*

This Reality-Show Gospel can sustain us for only so long. When we run out of reasons, we need something else entirely. We need each other.

There was a man named Job who understood that experience of *until*. He was an upstanding, generous neighbor. He was a great husband and father and boss. He was productive and a hard worker. He was faithful and holy. Even his body was in great shape. *Until*. Until painful, itchy boils erupted all over his skin. Until his herds of sheep and donkeys and cattle keeled over. Until his servants . . . and his sons . . . and his daughters were all killed. Until his life was totally upended. His sorrow outweighed all the sand in the sea (Job 6:3).

When Job's closest friends heard about all he had endured, they rushed to his side. They saw his shattered life and ripped their own clothes in shared grief. They sat with him, in the ashes, for seven days in silence. No words would help in the wake of such loss.

It was when they opened their mouths that they got themselves into trouble. They began spouting off the Ancient Near East's version of The Reality-Show Gospel (The Real Housewives of Uz, perhaps?). They attempted to give Job all the possible reasons why these bad things happened. *God is punishing you. If only you would repent. You are getting repaid for your sins or maybe those of your family.*

Eventually, Job is absolutely weary of them. "You are terrible at comforting me. Do you ever shut up?"*

It's so tempting to skip past the difficulty and pain and rush to find a rationale. But in the long pause, there is wisdom. Sometimes a reason isn't readily apparent, or perhaps it's not ours to assign. Job's friends got it right when they offered him the gift of their presence, but not the weight of their reasons.

So if you find yourself on the receiving end of these unhelpful clichés or are tempted to reach for them yourself, simmer down a bit. Instead, may you realize that you need to be reminded of how loved you are and that you are not alone. Even in this.

We need a warm hug. Long, lingering conversations. Small notes and gifts that make us feel known. And sometimes the best way to do that is by binge-watching *The Bachelor* together.

---

* Job 16:2–3, The Official Jessica Richie Translation

A Prayer for When You Don't Know What to Say

Blessed are you when you realize you are way out of your depth and you have no idea what to say. Blessed are you, confronted with suffering you can't imagine, but you don't say it. You do *not* say you can't imagine their pain, because you do want to imagine. You want to be there with them, in your heart and mind, imagining what they are feeling and what they might need.

Blessed are you there, silently, longing to bring comfort and ease. Your presence itself is prayer, and may the words that come be simple: I am so sorry. I love you. You are not alone.

Blessed are you who refuse to join the throng of the un-suffering. But choose instead to hurt beside those suffering. And love them right there without fixing or teaching or rescuing or bright-siding.

Blessed are you, there. In the love that waits for the dawn. *Amen.*

A GOOD ENOUGH STEP

Pick up the phone. Don't dial a number but speak out loud to an imagined person who has just told you about something terrible. Practice saying, "Oh, I'm so sorry." Then let yourself think of all the fixes that could be suggested, but don't say them. Then wonder in your head, *What can I do?* But not out loud. (You know they don't need the pressure.) Just say, "I'm coming your way and I have something I'll drop off." Then make a list of items you will stock up on, for just such a circumstance: little presents, cards, favorite snacks, a coffee gift card. Empathy and action. That's all you need.

WHAT *NOT* TO SAY TO A FRIEND IN NEED

"This would never have happened if you had your chakras
    adjusted as I suggested."
"Look on the bright side [insert many advantages of a
    lifetime of sorrow]."
"You poor dear. I'll be right over with my liver and prune
    casserole."
"When my grandmother caught that disease, the nurses said
    they'd never seen pustules that big before."
"It could have been worse. The alligator could have bitten off
    the hand you write with."

WHEN WORDS FAIL

Many of us are living in a strange, distended moment, the sameness of a world that groans for change. We need justice for all and miracles for the people we love. We need beauty that stirs our hearts and affordable health care for the parts of us that keep breaking.

There is hope for someday, but someday is not now.

There is a Christian version of this story. Holy Week begins with Jesus welcomed like a hero. Expectations are soaring: Jesus will fix everything. But by the end of the week, his best friends betray him, and he is convicted as a criminal and sentenced to death. He will rise from the dead and someday bring this world to a beautiful conclusion and wipe every tear from every eye.

There is hope for someday, but someday is not now.

And here we are, living between Good Friday and Easter Sunday. Before the cure. Or the answers you seek. Or the relationships and money you need. We live here before the heartbreak is over.

Perhaps it is here we might need to learn a new way to pray.

It's a way of paying attention that author Marilyn McEntyre calls "the subtle difference between listening *for* and listening *to*." It's an attitude of readiness without an agenda, an openness to what might come. Of breathing into a possibility of hearing and receiving something new.

Here, in poetic imagery, the mind is not pinned down like a butterfly under glass, but has wings to move unexpectedly. And McEntyre says that in her best times of listening prayer, this openness of heart allowed her to receive something she knew she hadn't "made up." It came as a gift.

This kind of special listening—listening as prayer—is something I experience sitting by the ocean.

I love the beach. It feels like settling under a weighted blanket. I can't be busy there, mostly because sand gets stuck under my laptop keys and is not easy to remove (trust me on this one). But little nagging thoughts are pulled away like waves peeling from the sand. There it comes again. And again. And this kind of listening is life-giving.

And it's there again when I read poetry, or listen to music.

As we sit there, perhaps we are waiting for miracles or hoping beyond hope. Perhaps we have often found ourselves without words. Perhaps here, our prayer can be a form of listening. Of paying attention to the world around us, watching for the presence of God that might come as a breeze or in a bird's song.

Life is not a pick-yourself-up-by-your-bootstraps enterprise. Sometimes you can't climb every mountain or swim every sea. But allowing ourselves to pause and listen steadies our anxious minds and unsettled hearts.

Listening for answers: *What should I love? How should I live?*

Maybe we won't know right away. And maybe it's okay to put our toes in the sand and allow the soundtrack of seagulls to quiet our thoughts and allow each crashing wave to be our prayer.

A Blessing for When You Might Not Know What to Pray . . . or Even Want To

Blessed are you, in the terrible wonderful now, fumbling around for the right words. You need so much, and it seems impossible to say it all. Blessed are you for whom prayer feels . . . hopeless. Disappointing. Futile.

Blessed are you in your radical honesty. In the ways you speak of your grief—the long sleepless nights in an empty bed. Of the physical pain you feel—the joints that don't work like they used to, your brain fog or chronic migraines. Blessed are you who speak of your loneliness, the empty home or nest or womb. Who have the audacity to ask for the miracles you need. The healing or a new friend or a redeemed family.

Blessed are you as you learn to trust. Trust a God who hears, who listens, who hasn't left your side. Who prays on your behalf, interpreting those deep groans you can't quite put into syllables or sounds.

Blessed are you as you settle into acceptance. Blessed are we who live here . . . in the someday but not yet.

A GOOD ENOUGH STEP

It's no secret that urban living, splendid in some ways, has its drawbacks. Noise, concrete, and congestion are not conducive to a light heart and a merry step. This is especially true in our day and age, which keeps us glued to our screens. There is a movement of people who are trying to convince people to find renewal outside. The Japanese call it *shinrin-yoku;* Germans call it *Waldbaden.* It's "forest bathing," the new trend in ecotherapy that promises to improve your health and mental well-being while you stroll through the woods.

Proponents of forest bathing urge you to step back into the wilderness. They want us to undertake not a purposeful hike, but a slow walk through trees and greenery, using all our senses to refresh our mind and body: to notice the different types of grasses, feel the breeze on our skin, listen to the birdcalls. Some doctors claim it boosts immune systems. Artists say the walks spur their creativity. I think we can all agree that listening to the silence of nature rightsizes us and whatever it is we are facing.

Take a bath in the forest today. Maybe you don't have a forest accessible; a park will do. Even a walk through the neighborhood. Or plop yourself by a stream or lake or ocean. No need to speak. Let the natural sounds around you be your prayer.

"God speaks in the silence of the heart. Listening is the beginning of prayer." —attr. MOTHER TERESA

2:00 A.M./2:00 P.M.

There is no small talk at two o'clock in the morning.

If you're at a party, you find yourself saying: "Oh, totally! That's exactly what happened to me when [insert long, incredibly disclosive story you'll wish tomorrow you hadn't said]."

If you're on the phone, you can hear yourself saying things you would *never* say in the light of day. *I always hated that about myself. Do you think I can change? And why didn't anyone tell me that my face can't sustain the wow factor of bangs?*

Most often you've woken up and stared bleary-eyed at the ceiling while every fear comes flooding back. Your health. Your relationship or singleness. Your kids. The people come and gone. Bills and errands and existential threats to tomorrow. *God, I can't do this much longer.*

So often, we forget our 2:00 A.M. selves. We are someone else entirely: our 2:00 P.M. selves. The momentum of the day is carrying us through our work and errands, and we have begun to believe that productivity and mental feats of efficiency are entirely within our control. It's a wonderful, fleeting feeling and our checklist minds are pleased as punch. We are unstoppable! We can survive multitasking! Bring it on, universe. I'm ready.

There was a long stretch of time when I was entirely a 2:00 P.M. person. I was young and clever and ignorant of the way that we have stretches of wholeness and ones of fracture. I had not entirely realized a hard truth of living, that for many people, carrying on, for days and weeks and months, will feel like an existential struggle to simply keep living. For them, it's always 2:00 A.M.

There's a moment I will never forget that seared that reality in my mind. I was in the midst of a long stretch of chemotherapy that required me to get on an airplane in the middle of the night. By dawn I had landed in another city where I would prepare to spend the rest of the day having poison pumped efficiently into my veins before I returned to my own city and my own bed after midnight. It was grueling. My skin was sallow and thin, my nerves frayed. But every Wednesday I would do it all over again.

One Wednesday, I began to notice that I was not alone in my routine. In the Atlanta airport, in a sea of strangers, I started to see familiar faces. A woman and her two kids curled around her feet sleeping on their coats. Another family dragging their belongings around in luggage, hoping, I'm sure, they would look like they too had stepped off a plane. But there, in the airport bathroom, I began to see them: the haggard mother washing her child's face in the sink. Smoothing his hair. Placing a hand on his cheek. They were sleeping at the airport, trying to find the resources to get their children to school on time and to face another day.

Once we know pain, it is like the dark side of the moon. Hidden from view, but every bit as real.

The world is full of 2:00 A.M. people. It is me. It is you. So we reach out to hold hands in the dark.

A Blessing for When You See Things as They Always Were

Blessed are you who see it all now. The terrible, beautiful truth that our world, our lives seem irreparably broken. And you can't unsee it. The hungry kid. The exhausted mom. The woman who wonders if any of this is worth it. The loneliness and despair.

Blessed are you who glimpse reality and don't turn away. This kind of seeing comes at a steep cost, and it is a cost you may not have paid intentionally, but here you are. Seeing things clearly. Blessed are you who have worked hard to keep your heart soft. You who live with courage, fixing what is in your reach, praying about what is not, and loving, still.

May you experience deeper capacity and glimpses of hope, as you continue to see the world as it is. Terrible. Beautiful. Fragile.

A GOOD ENOUGH STEP

Perform a bit of dislocated exegesis. This is a Bible study tactic that makes you move out of your normal place of reading and see what new observations come up because of your new surroundings. Read Isaiah 40:1–26 outside and after the sun has gone to bed. You might need a flashlight or to pull it up on your phone. Read it once quietly. Then again aloud, slowly. What do you notice about the passage? How do your surroundings inform what it means to you?

"During the day it is hard to remember that all the stars in the sky are out there all the time, even when I am too blinded by the sun to see them."

—BARBARA BROWN TAYLOR, *Learning to Walk in the Dark*

THE IN-BETWEEN

We like to pretend that our lives are marked by consistency, durability. *I'm a mom. I work here. These are my friends and my loved ones, and this is the book club I don't ever read the books for.* And yet we find ourselves *between* realities.

Between relationships.
Between seasons of independence and dependence.
Between jobs.
Between friends.
Between the diagnosis and cure.
Between feeling courageous and feeling afraid.
Between the life we have . . . and the life we want.

The anthropologist Victor Turner wrote about what happens when people go through intense change together, and referred to the in-between time as "liminality." We are at a threshold—something still becoming—but we don't know yet what all the factors are, and how to frame them. We yearn for normalcy only to find that liminality has become our "new normal."

Life itself is a liminal state, and learning how to live requires the remedy that Jesus came to offer. He said that if you lose your life for His sake, you will gain it (Matthew 10:39). So little is in our control, but then again, so little ever was. The living and breathing and struggling and crying and teaching and trying and dying. This is the life we have, in skin and bones, living.

Liminality is also a place where we are not yet settled. Not yet solidified. Exposed is one way to put it. But also open to something new.

So let's take a minute here, in the in-between.

Sometimes when we feel lost, floating outside of what we know, who we wanted to be and where we wanted to be, it's tempting to feel small and wonder . . . maybe. Maybe I should just shut this down a bit.

Maybe no one needs to hear from me. Maybe that's enough for now.

So my loves, bless you if you are there, in that place that is in between.

In-between can be an awfully lonely place. In transition, exposed, that place of waiting and vulnerability. A place that doesn't fit anyone's idea of normal because there aren't words for it, and it isn't there yet.

Instead of trying to escape it, let us settle there for the moment. Knowing and trusting we aren't alone. We're in this strange middle place . . . together.

A Blessing for the In-Between

Blessed are we, somewhere unnameable, fully present to our reality. Tracking it, with all its subtle gradations and colors and contrasts, the sweetness and the struggle, the stuck and not-quite-fitting. Authentic to it, mapping the full strangeness of the new emergent landscape.

Blessed are we, dear ones, not calling it too soon. Not settling for the neat and buttoned-up, the too-tied-up, the not-quite-true.

Bless all of it, the way we might widen our gaze to encompass it and embrace it. And bless you, moving into the unknown, waiting, daring to hope.

A GOOD ENOUGH STEP

Remember the last time you got your eyes tested? And you read out the letters on the smallest line you could see. Then your optometrist asked you, "Which is clearer, one . . . or two?" and you paused and you wondered. And before you answered, she flipped back to one and you knew then, right away. It's one. And it's such a relief to know for sure. But the in-between is not so comfortable. However, it's where we live most of the time. So here's the deal. For one hour, consent to the in-between. Nestle right in there, not knowing anything for sure. Crazy, isn't it? That's not where we are comfortable. But try it for one solid hour. Not straining for answers. Not pushing to land an idea. Or solve a problem. See if a poem or song fits. Or maybe Psalm 131:

"My heart is not proud, Lord,
My eyes are not lifted up,
I do not occupy myself with things too great and
    marvelous for me.
But I have calmed and quieted my soul, like a weaned
    child with its mother
My soul is like a weaned child within me.
Oh Israel, trust in the Lord, from this time forth, and even
    forever more." (Psalm 131:1–3)

And if you do happen to get a nudge where something comes clear, a just-noticeable difference—sometimes the shift comes sideways, the truth that something has changed—receive it. And if not, just rest awhile in the unknowing. Because someday we will see things as they really are. You can count on it.

"I wanted a perfect ending. Now I've learned, the hard way, that some poems don't rhyme, and some stories don't have a clear beginning, middle, and end. Life is about not knowing, having to change, taking the moment and making the best of it, without knowing what's going to happen next. Delicious ambiguity."   —GILDA RADNER, in *Navigate the Chaos in 2020*

TOO FEW SPARROWS

Hominem unius libri timeo. It's a wonderful phrase attributed to everyone from the ancient Stoic Seneca to the medieval theologian Thomas Aquinas, but it's a fabulous warning: "Beware the man of a single book." Beware of the person who has a totalizing view. Don't simply watch out for people who seem to be narrow-minded—look for the person who thinks they have a single explanation for everything. After all, we must consider the sparrows.

In 1958, the communist Chinese government of Mao Zedong declared war on the nation's sparrows, declaring that these "birds are the public animals of capitalism," eating up precious seed grain. A massive campaign of noise was launched to keep the birds constantly in flight and dying of exhaustion. In the fields and cities, drums were ceaselessly pounded upon, pots and pans were beaten, fireworks were set off and before too long the little birds began to fall from the sky in great numbers. In the capital city, Beijing, sparrows found refuge on the grounds of foreign embassies, which refused to allow the noisy mobs entrance, but the buildings were surrounded by cacophonous groundskeepers who kept up a constant assault. This tactic was so successful that workers at the Polish embassy had to use shovels to clear the precinct of dead sparrows. China was victorious in its war, and soon the numbers of live birds had reached extinction levels.

Within two years, however, it was noted that the rice harvest had actually decreased. In the absence of sparrows, the insects they had fed upon had multiplied and attacked crops. Plagues of locusts went unchecked and exacerbated a horrible famine that ended up killing tens of millions of Chinese citizens. To revive the sparrow population, the government was forced to import 250,000 birds from the Soviet Union.

Perhaps there were too many sparrows. But a single solution was not a solution at all.

So often, we are people of a single book. We read only a single news source or listen to only one friend before making up our minds. We may think we have considered all the options, but, more and more, we associate with people who are in mental lockstep. We didn't mean to be this way, but if someone mentions a complicated moral issue, we can hear ourselves spouting well-polished talking points. We do less listening and more browbeating other arguments into submission.

To be fair, yes, everyone is judging you. You will be too liberal or too conservative, too radical or too permissive, too slow or too rash. You have not performed your integrity to anyone's satisfaction, and *we have been talking about it.*

We all know people on social media whose primary mode of interaction is denouncement. This is not "faith seeking understanding." This is a heat-seeking missile of blame.

This is a time of intense political polarization and misinformation with few common sources of media and shared discourse. And as the culture wars rage on and we feel the tremors of the ground beneath our feet, we are constantly at risk of becoming monocausal in our accounts of the world and each other. We must re-commit to a larger vision of life together without much agreement.

If we are going to be the kind of people who build a more equitable world, work toward peace, and fight for justice, there must be room for anger and lament. But how will we know when we're on the right track? We can search for the signs—there will be love, joy, peace, patience, kindness, goodness, gentleness, faithfulness, and self-control. Those are the gifts of the Spirit which remind us that God is truly present.

So, let's beware of being the man of a single book. Applying one principle, solution, or belief with a singu-larity that dominates all other considerations is to browbeat other arguments into submission. Let's act boldly and with purpose, checking always to see what's in our hand. If it seems more like a club or a stick, set it down.

A Blessing for Being Open to Change

Blessed are we, the ones who have just discovered that others might not look at things the way we do—and maybe they have a point. Just maybe.

Blessed are we, the newly wrong, chuckling over how much it hurts to be chastened a little. Blessed are we realizing that our fixes for others might actually be mirrors to hold up first for ourselves. And blessed are we, seeing that You, Lord, desire our good above all, we give You our worship and praise through our readiness to pivot according to Your direction.

Our hearts are soft, our ears open. Speak, Lord, of the change You desire to write into our life stories as they unfold. For we are gently becoming aware that knowledge will not be the basis for our understanding of how life goes. Love will. *Amen.*

A GOOD ENOUGH STEP

Let's try this in a fun way. For a moment, try weaponized piety. "Dear God, thank You that I am not like my enemies." Say it as loudly as you want and feel free to use names. I'm thinking of a few people as we speak. Allow the humor and truth and sanctimoniousness of those words to shake us up and loosen the grip of weaponized piety on us. Now try again. "Dear God, I believe so much in [insert cause or justice or policy], how might I bring the truth of this into action?"

Jesus gives us a little test to know whether someone is doing good. It's during one of his long-winded speeches recorded in Matthew's Gospel: the Sermon on the Mount. He says, "Beware of false prophets, who come to you in sheep's clothing, but inwardly they are ravenous wolves. You will know them by their fruits. Do men gather grapes from thornbushes or figs from thistles? Even so, every good tree bears good fruit, but a bad tree bears bad fruit. A good tree cannot bear bad fruit, nor *can* a bad tree bear good fruit. Every tree that does not bear good fruit is cut down and thrown into the fire. Therefore, by their fruits you will know them" (Matthew 7:15–20). What fruit is being produced? Is it good? Rotten? Prickly? The metaphor ends there, but we can guess what makes fruit good is that which looks like Jesus. Loving. Joyful. Peacemaking. Long-suffering. Kind. Good. Gentle. Faithful. Self-restrained.

39

BRIGHT HOPE

have a hard time navigating my relationship with hope. Sure, I hope for healed bodies and restored families, an end to mass shootings and no need for war. But, just as I can imagine a better future, a news story or my Twitter feed bursts my optimism, sending me crashing back to earth, back to reality where hope is a dangerous word.

Too much hope, and you are, frankly, delusional. Too little hope, and you will drown in despair. So, how do we have hope when our reality looks so hopeless?

There is this obscure book of the Bible that shows up in the lectionary only a handful of times, and you will rarely hear someone talk about it because, let's face it, it's pretty strange.

Ezekiel was a prophet and a priest chosen by God to explain his reality. The Babylonians, led by King Nebuchadnezzar, had removed the Judeans from their land, taken them into captivity, and marched them hundreds of miles into exile. Ezekiel was only twenty-five. They probably didn't have adequate shoes, food, or shelter for the long journey. In Jewish thought at the time, the Temple was the location of the divine, so to be removed from that sacred site meant being removed from God's presence. What's more, several years into captivity, Jerusalem was sacked. The temple was destroyed. God was gone.

Ezekiel was a traumatized witness to a traumatized people.

His strange visions and dreams grapple with the horrors they experienced. People dying. People ripped from their homes. People separated from those they loved. People abandoned by God. He bore witness to the not-yet-ness. The unknowing of when this would end. The totalizing feeling of despair. The depth of un-hope.

But then something odd happened.

Ezekiel stood over a mass grave. Under his feet were thousands of dry bones. It might have been an old battlefield, or perhaps the Judeans taken into captivity weren't allotted individual burials, their decaying bodies tossed in a trash heap.

Then God Almighty asked Ezekiel a really stupid question: *Can these bones live?*

I can only imagine how despairing he felt, standing over the bodies of loved ones. Cousins. Neighbors. Friends. His own wife. Too many to count. Wartime doesn't offer the luxury of funerals. Neither do pandemics.

Ezekiel was looking at death close up as bones disintegrated under his toes. If you ever have witnessed death, you know how infuriating it is to be asked the question: *Can these bones live?* Of course not.

What good is hope in this place, spoken over a pile of drying bones?

God asked Ezekiel to prophesy that God would resurrect the dead. That God would restore a community. That God would establish a kingdom. That God would build the temple. That God would put bones back together. That all hope is not lost.

Then, the vision continued. Ezekiel felt rattling under his toes. Cartilage cracked together. Ligaments were sewn. Skin stretched. Lungs filled with the very breath of God. The Valley of Dry Bones rushed with life once again.

God is not done yet. When all we see is death and decay and destruction and disease, God sees hope, but not an empty optimism or empty phrase. God sees hard-won hope. Hope with feet. Hope that takes work.

Can these bones live?

But the restoration of Israel doesn't come without the participation of her people. This isn't about standing passively by while they watch God work. Ezekiel goes on to narrate how Israel will be restored. The land and the people that he thought were destroyed forever will be restored because the people will build a new temple. The people will establish a new polity. The people will rebuild.

The people of God will work alongside God to restore the land.

After describing God's vision for Israel's restoration,